CW00871811

CONTENTS

The planet does not need
more "successful people."
The planet desperately needs
more peacemakers, healers,
restorers, storytellers
and lovers of all kinds.

— DALAI LAMA

ACKNOWLEDGEMENT

During my career as a Clinical Hypnotherapist and training provider, I have been honoured and privileged to meet some amazing caring, compassionate people who have contributed to my life's goal to help one million people before I die!

It's not been easy. I remember the advice given to me over twenty years ago from a man I still have not had the pleasure to actually meet in person. William Broom, who at that time was founder of General Hypnotherapy Standards Council offered the following advice as he wished me well with my new found career.

"Brian, the more successful you become, the more enemies you will make, but don't let them hold you back!"

Well, that was probably the best advice anyone could have given me and by far the most accurate. Little did I know that this career would bring enemies. Fortunately by the few!

Bill has over the years continued to support Innervisions through good times and bad and for this I am eternally grateful.

I would also like to portray gratitude to all the people who agreed to write a contribution towards this book. And to those who forgave me for pressurising them to meet deadlines.

And finally to my life partner Shirley who relentlessly offered her Microsoft skills to help me format the pages and upload the data to Creatspace so that the book could meet their publishing requirements.

FOREWARD: KATHRYN LAING

I met Brian way back in 2007 when I was looking for a career change and enrolled on the Innervisions Clinical Hypnosis course and we have become firm friends ever since.

The first thing that struck me about Brian was his absolute love and passion for the subject and over a short period of time it was clear that his method of teaching was really quite unique firstly in that we were to avoid generic scripts and learn how to connect with a person and make their experience very personal to them. His wealth of knowledge in the subject and vast experience were second to none and his delivery always edged with his wicked sense of humour.

Brian has a fascinating back story (which he shares openly with people), yet despite his troubled start in life, Brian's gritty determination always shone through and he eventually went on to train to become a stage hypnotist. This career was a huge success with time spent as the resident stage hypnotist on Blackpool's Central Pier. But over time Brian began to realise just how powerful hypnosis could be when he used his knowledge to help mend his own arm which had been severely damaged and paralysed in an accident. This then prompted Brian to re-train as a clinical hypnotherapist going on to help countless people over many years.

Shamed by his past, Brian struggled for some time and eventually vowed to help a million people during his lifetime.

Armed with this wealth of experience, Brian wanted to be able to share his skill and knowledge as part of his quest to reach his target million, and train others to also become hypnotherapists – hence 'Innervisions' was born.

After completing my own course with Brian I had the privilege to work alongside him as co-tutor and witnessed so many people, from all walks of life, transform their lives to also become successful clinical hypnotherapists, many of whom lacked their own confidence, self-esteem for whatever reasons yet conquered and went forth (a fabulous side effect experienced by many on the course). Most of whom are now actively contributing to Brian's million by seeing clients on a daily basis in their own private practice.

Brian continues to work with clients from all walks of life, teach, and has also gone on to train trainers to teach his unique hypnotherapy training course on his behalf. Also a keen advocate of The Law of Attraction (a subject he has taught and written on extensively), Brian, along with the collaboration and contribution from past students has now published this (his fourth book) to help inspire others in this wonderful and fascinating profession and perhaps contribute towards that million! Enjoy.

INTRODUCION

In February 2017 I celebrated twenty one years as a Hypnotherapy Training provider. I conducted my very first training course in the East Yorkshire town of Goole back in 1996

It actually all started twenty five years ago, when I changed direction and became a clinical hypnotherapist sparked by an amazing insight inspired by my father whilst performing my hypnosis stage act on Blackpool Pier.

I had recently been disabled by an industrial injury where my dominant right arm was paralysed and withering away. My positive nature found a way to come to terms with my doctor's advice to amputate my arm, I was then actually looking forward to this in anticipation of being recognised as 'the one armed hypnotist' – I even had posters printed!

My father commented on the power of the mind after attending my stage show and inspired me to use the power of my mind to repair my paralysed right arm. An amazing light bulb moment.

I studied the works of Milton Erickson MD who on two separate occasions used the power of his mind to learn to walk again following paralysis caused by polio.

The following twelve months was a turning point in my life as I used my skills to bring my arm back to around 95% recovery. I considered the industrial accident to be Karmic debt due to my rather aggressive and colourful teenage years, and spent time looking for a way to neutralise that debt. Then a few weeks later I woke in the earlier hours of the morning with an amazing inspirational and overwhelming message. It was in that moment that I made an agreement with myself which would eventually serve as my life's purpose whilst at the same time neutralise the Karmic debt I had accumulated as a teenager.

This was my revelation.

MY LIFE'S PURPOSE:
TO HELP ONE MILLION PEOPLE BEFORE I DIE...

And so it began, my life became meaningful; for the first time in my life I have a sense of purpose. I abandoned stage hypnosis, attended a basic hypnotherapy training course and opened my first hypnotherapy clinic. I also enrolled on an 'A' level psychology course at my local college which eventually lead me to a degree in clinical psychology.

Miracles started to happen right before my eyes. I was seeing clients on a daily basis after opening a complimentary Health Centre on Hessle Road Hull.

Still not feeling like I was doing enough to achieve my Million, I decided to teach other people to do the work that I did creating a pyramid effect. This led to the birth of my training company, **Innervisions School of Clinical Hypnosis.**

Established in 1996, Innervisions School of Clinical Hypnosis is now the training provider of choice providing specialised training in modern clinical hypnosis at various locations around the UK and Spain.

Now semi-retired from hypnotherapy, and running the business from our beautiful home in the Costa Blanca region of Spain, I am privileged and honoured to have a fantastic and wonderful team of dedicated tutors working at various venues around the UK and also here in Spain.

Behind the scenes, I have my wonderful and loving partner, Shirley, keeping me motivated and in good spirits doing all the business related stuff that I don't like doing!

Welcome to the fascinating and wonderful world of modern clinical hypnosis. I hope you enjoy the contents of this book!

Take care, stay safe, and enjoy this book. And perhaps you too could become part of my million!

With love...

BRIAN GLENN: PRINCIPAL – INNERVISIONS SCHOOL OF CLINICAL HYPNOSIS

HYPNOTHERAPY

Hypnotherapy is using the state of hypnosis to treat a variety of medical and psychological problems. It is estimated that 85% of people will respond at some level to clinical hypnotherapy. It may even succeed where other more conventional methods of treatment have not produced the desired result. When carried out by a trained and qualified hypnotherapist the benefits can be long lasting and often permanent. It is natural and safe, with no harmful side effects.

Hypnotherapy makes use of the bicameral nature of the functioning brain and the conscious/unconscious processes therein. At its simplest level the unconscious mind becomes (through our life experience) the repository of our conditioned experience, while the conscious mind is the waking mind dealing with appraisal and decision making. In hypnotherapy the critical faculties of the conscious mind are sidestepped (through the hypnotic condition) and new ideas and 'suggestions' placed directly into the uncritical unconscious to effect beneficial changes when back in the waking state.

TO BE A HYPNOTHERAPIST.

Well it's not really about swinging watches and dancing like a chicken! It may be surprising to many to learn that we experience trance states often during the course of our lives. Even passing into ordinary sleep involves a kind of trance state. The experience of hypnosis is similar. Neither asleep nor awake, and a little like daydreaming, with a pleasant feeling of deep relaxation behind it all. Hypnosis is a different state of consciousness which you can naturally enter so that, for therapeutic purposes (hypnotherapy), beneficial corrections may be given directly to your unconscious mind.

In this way, hypnosis is an effective way of making contact with our inner (unconscious) self, which is both a reservoir of unrecognized potential and knowledge as well as being the unwitting source of many of our problems.

Realistically no-one can be hypnotized against their will and even when hypnotised, a person can still reject any suggestion. Thus hypnotherapy could be considered to be a state of purposeful co-operation.

CHARACTER

Some of the traits that are conducive to being a good hypnotherapist are not related to social class, age, disabilities, education, qualifications, religion etc. But more a humanistic and empathic approach to life. Hypnotherapists should behave like hypnotherapists and offer love, respect, forgives and compassion as much in their personal and private lives as they do in there therapeutic setting.

Just a few days ago I was chatting with a lady on a plane journey back to Spain and the discussion came round to the paradigm of 'world peace'. She spent a while explaining how we all should live peacefully, and in harmony, and a world united. Then as the conversation progressed she ended up telling me how she fell out with her next door neighbour over a year ago due to her views on Brexit!

World peace really needs to begin in our own hearts!

Some of the best lessons we ever learn, we learn from our mistakes and failures. The errors of the past are the success and wisdom of our future.

If we make our goal to live a life of compassion and unconditional love, then the world will indeed become a garden where all kinds of flowers can bloom and grow.

One forgives as much as one loves.

Learn to get in touch with the silence within yourself and know that everything in this life has a purpose. Live every day as if it was your last because the future belongs to those who believe in the beauty of their dreams!

Take time to notice and appreciate the tiny miracles around you, and feel content in the now!

Accept that you cannot change another person, let others be who they are and simply love who you are! It is not up to you to take responsibility for others!

If you can make even a small difference to someone's life, you'll start making a difference to your own life too. We are all part of a wonderful journey!

When you get into a tight place and everything goes against you, till it seems as though you could not hang on a minute longer, never give up, for that is just the place and time that the tide will turn! Even a mistake may turn out to be the one thing necessary to a worthwhile achievement!

Remember that whatever feelings you have within you are attracting your tomorrow.

Worry attracts more worry. Anxiety attracts more anxiety. Unhappiness attracts more unhappiness. Dissatisfaction attracts more dissatisfaction.

And...

Joy attracts more joy. Happiness attracts more happiness. Peace attracts more peace. Gratitude attracts more gratitude. Kindness attracts more kindness. Love attracts more love.

Your job is an inside one. To change your world, all you have to do is change the way you feel inside.

How easy is that?

(Whatever your answer is, you are right)

GAYNOR MARIE DUFFY: BUTTERFLY'S AND MATCHSTICKS

As she lights the next match, she sees a vision of her grandmother, the only person to have treated her with love and kindness all through her life. To keep the vision of her grandmother alive for as long as she can, the girl lights the entire bundle of matches at once.

After running out of matches the child dies and her grandmother carries her soul to Heaven. The next morning, passers-by find the girl dead in the nook, frozen with a smile on her face, and guess the reason for the burnt-out matches beside her. They feel pity for her, although they had not shown kindness to her before her death. They have no way of knowing about the wonderful visions she saw before her death or how gloriously she is celebrating the New Year in Heaven with her grandmother.

The little match girl by HANS CHRISTIAN ANDERSON.

Just like the 'little match girl we all have the ability tune into our imagination and as a child I used to imagine a family filled with kindness and love and as I lay on a makeshift bed (an old sofa picked up from a scrap yard) I used to search in the arms of the sofa for this family. The people were made from the spent matches that my heavy smoking Father cast aside. They were my secret family and as the candle light cast its shadows from another 1970's power strike, I would imagine the life that I would one day live with my matchstick family.

BEFORE BECOMING A HYPNOTHERAPIST

Before becoming a hypnotherapist I had a life which I would divide into three parts... which I believe have been an influencing factor to becoming a hypnotherapist.

The first part as a child is where, I suppose, everybody's first part of life starts. During my time as a child I would immerse myself in the imaginary world of Enid Blyton and Hans Christian Anderson. The excerpt from the book above portrays the dying hopes and dreams of the little matchstick girl, and was always one of my all-time favourite books. However, I always felt sad that the girl had to die in order to achieve her hopes and dreams. As a child, I was always optimistic and knew that I would achieve my hopes and dreams... even in the most difficult circumstances. Yet as an adult I have, at times, lost sight of this natural use of my imagination and use of my subconscious.

In the second part of my life and before becoming a hypnotherapist I lived a happy life with the matchstick family that I imagined in my childhood. I worked in different jobs. office worker, cleaner, a bank worker and waitress and was the typical mundane housewife, doing the school run, cleaning the house, making sure the kids did their homework and juggling part-time work to fit in with my husband's job and my household duties.

In this second part of my life back in 1998, I had just given birth to my third child, which my two boys now refer to as the birth of 'a real-life princess'. During that year, I lived a floaty life living upon a cloud with my beautiful matchstick family reflecting on how wonderful my life was. Unbeknown to me in those early stages in 1998, living the reality of life amidst Bill Clinton denying his affair with Monica Lewinsky, Osama Bin Laden publishing his fatwa , Saving Private Ryan pitching the top spot at the Cinemas and a brim-full of Asha resonating from our radios, my life was slowly started to spiral out of control and the matchstick family I had created had no idea what the hell was going on.

To be honest, I am not even sure when the anxiety first started creeping up on me, but from being a normal sociable person, I soon found myself making excuses not to go out and slowly started to become uncomfortable and fearful with everything around me. Firstly, I was just worrying about things on the television and becoming concerned that this would impact on my children's wellbeing. At other times I would worry that the children would get some terrible illness. At its pinnacle I was wakening in the night, refusing to leave the house, being sick, running constantly to the toilet and struggling to breathe at almost any situation. Quite literally my life had become controlled by fear and I did not know what to do about it. Being a private person I kept it to myself, not even confiding in my husband or family. Eventually, I broke down to my sister in law and agreed to visit the doctor.

A visit to my GP revealed panic attacks and one night whilst relaxing in the bath and reflecting on my situation I suddenly realised I am doing this to me! This might seem obvious now, but this was 1998 and introspective thinking was not something you did in working-class Manchester. Further reading took me to books rather than pills. And eventually searched out a hypnotherapist. Even though I innately felt that this sort of therapy would help I could not help feeling uneasy about the prospect of visiting a hypnotherapist. The media's false perception of the watch swinging hypnotherapist I had seen in films made me feel slightly uncomfortable.

Back in 1998 that was the way I thought about hypnotherapy and after feeling nervous on my first session, I was pleasantly surprised that I was aware of everything around me, even though I was in an extremely relaxed state. I had a number of sessions of hypnotherapy, which revealed some issues from my past, but it did enable me to see that I could not escape a past that was and always had been part of who I was. A past that I had for over 20 years, decided to close my conscious mind too.

Now in this second stage of my life, it appeared that my childhood had impacted on my happy matchstick life. This surprised me because as working-class Manchester lass, born in the 1960s and growing up in the 70's and 80's it was something that we were told not to dwell on. I grew up in the streets of 'let's have it!' In a family of 'Our kid'. Well, actually there were nine other 'Our kids'. As a child, I worked from 12 years old to bring £2.00 home to buy bread Jam and biscuits for Sunday tea. During these years I hardly attended school and was an educational statistic of the era. A working-class subculture, a girl who was expected to grow up achieving nothing academically.

Prior to my working class normality, I had lived in deprivation in Newton Heath and had lost my Mother and brother in a house fire. My sisters and I were lucky enough to be thrown from a bedroom window. Apparently a year after the fire I did not speak a word. This is bizarre because I can vividly recall living quite contently in a world of my imagination hoping that the people in the outside world would just disappear. At that time I was in no way aware of the concerns of the adults around me, although I would occasionally hear the adult voices making concerned comments about how they worried about my living in a dream world. Apart from that I was ignored and left to live in the world of my imagination and that was ok, because quite frankly I was alright and it was a good place to be.

Within 6 months of the fire, my Dad remarried and we were placed under the care of our mentally unstable stepmother. A typical 1970s, Manchester upbringing I suppose. We subsequently went on to experience physical and mental abuse, ranging from burning our fingers on the open flame of a gas stove, to my sister being locked naked in a coal shed, with no food for days. This was eventually reported to social services by the neighbours, which involved the police and my sister leaving home. At the age of 14, I eft the hell house and slept rough as a little street urchin until the neighbours phoned the police and I was picked up. There were moments when it was suggested that I might spend my childhood in a children's home. Thankfully reports in a newspaper alerted a kind Auntie and Uncle and they conversed with my Father, who within hours traded me in for a child allowance weekly payment of £5.25, leaving me to lead a happy life and closing the door to my subconscious mind.

Well, that was not quite it, as I went on to be a little shit... was very disruptive in school and had extreme attitude and behaviour that make today's teenagers look like kittens. In retrospect I probably could have ended up in a care-home, but thankfully the kind Auntie and Uncle were patient and although I left school with not a qualification to speak of. By the age of 19 had got my shit together stopped putting two fingers up to the world and went on to live my matchstick life.

Well, enter the third part of my life, after 1998, which was a kick up the backside for me. The waiting had gone on long enough and I had to move on with my life. The truth was I was ashamed of my life as a child. Seriously, it is embarrassing to admit that you had no significance as a child to anybody, a none-entity. Unlike the little match, girl I had refused to die clinging to the happy memories, I was proud of my working class resilience, so I had shut the door. Yet now this third stage of my life had given me a whole new perspective, which was how to create some good in the world from my experiences. What was I thinking? No way on earth could I live the life of suburbia and expect my subconscious not to come knocking. The experience gave me an understanding of fear and I swore never to experience this type of fear again. This was a turning point and I went on a journey to push myself in order that I would never experience anxiety or fear again.

After the experience with anxiety and subsequent hypnotherapy I had a whole new attitude. The minute I felt churning in my stomach I would push myself to go above and beyond. Within four years I had completed and achieved a 2:1 English and History degree at Manchester University. If I am honest during that time I felt like a fish out of the water, as I worked with what I called two-dimensional people, who were at the University. It was wrong to think that way, but these were people from middle-class families who were articulate and able to express themselves. These were people who the world would listen too. Often there were times when I felt...'who am I kidding'? Nevertheless, I just felt that I had to keep pushing myself. I felt it was a means to an end to using my past to change the world.

After achieving my degree I went on to complete a two year PGCE in teaching Design and Technology as I perceived that my life was to work with those kids whose lives were like mine. Working class kids with low aspirations who dreamed of having and living happy matchstick lives. Was it easy? Hell no! I had achieved nothing at school and now I was supposed to put academic essays together. At times my anxiety was through the roof. After getting the kids ready for school I cried like a baby driving to university, but every night I did my self-hypnosis, which I had read about in books. Going down the stairs of my mind I went into my subconscious to a place and let balloons go to release anxiety, drank cocktails of confidence and when I felt I could not complete my academic studies I went to a place where I strutted around with a mortarboard on my head. At the time I did not even know the name of it, but just imagined that it would give me intelligence and in many ways, I suppose it did give me the drive and hope to complete my degree.

In 2006 I finished my degree and decided upon a teaching qualification and would eventually wear the mortarboard three times in reality. One for my degree, once for my PGCE degree and one for a masters that I completed in 2011.

After reading 'The Secret', by Rhonda Byrne, 2009, my imagination was alighted with manifestation and becoming a useful member of society. Still interested in changing the life of working-class children and their outcomes in society I visited the local courts. These visits revealed that the children whose lives had been impacted by poor social and economic environments and poor education would often end up in court and in prison. After visiting the court, eventually the staff suggested that I be put forward as a magistrate and I agreed. From 2006 to 2014 I became a magistrate in the youth court in a hope to understand and improve the life chances of young people.

Eventually, qualifying as a teacher in 2009, an opportunity presented itself within the school I taught to complete a funded Masters. In 2011, still in an attempt to make life changes to the children, I completed a master about working-class children. The fact I achieved a distinction was not that impressive as I was actually speaking about what I knew and had lived and enjoyed the research. Eventually, I was asked to go to London to speak about the issues with working-class children in education and a housing magazine asked for my input on education. This was presented as the riot report in 2012

'Do you fancy going to a hypnotherapy course with me next weekend', one of my colleagues shouted to me as I rushed past her to my next lesson. I decided to catch her later to find out what she meant. That evening I went to the link on the internet that she passed onto me and I read through the course details. Some of the things seemed fascinating and I had experienced ten sessions of hypnotherapy 18 years before. I could not get the thought of the course out of my head as the hypnotherapy I had experienced had been life changing and was intrigued to look at it from a contrasting perspective.

The truth was I was just so unfulfilled within education! Why? Because although I was working with young people, the education system had turned these students into pieces of data. Changes in education had teachers completing realms and realms of data, paperwork and the staff turnover was horrific due to the political intervention of government and constant changes. Whilst working in education I had at times tried to get working class children involved with community projects, but the reality of teaching was now making this more and more difficult. Yes the results of the students I taught were good, but as I witnessed a decline in staff and student wellbeing I questioned what we were all really learning.

The fact was I had now started to debate whether being in education was the place for me to make the changes I felt compelled to make and be really fulfilled. Whilst completing my masters in 2011 reading and research had given me a good understanding of the political influences in education and how a university education was creating overqualified young people with no jobs to go to. At that time I also learned about the Pisa tables and how the government was competing with other countries to make Britain's educational system the best in the world. Sounds good, but the problem was that the so-called best in the world were countries like China, Singapore, and Korea also has the highest child suicide rates. Stories emerged of how children lived in anxiety telling parents if test results were less than 90%. My research revealed that an effort to compete globally, governments place extreme academic pressure onto children. These children are missing out on a more holistic education such as play, social and motor skills. Mental health had become a huge issue in our education system amongst teaching staff and students and I felt the dissatisfaction of this. Was I making the difference that I so needed to make? No! I now felt that I was part of the problem.

In addition to all of this I had completed my masters in 2011 and the then Headmaster read the masters and took on some of my recommendations. The recommendations in my masters had been that working-class children, should have more after-school activities. The truth had been that over the years funding had been cut and many of the youth clubs and working lads clubs had closed down. One of my good friends and colleagues read my masters and immediately started to put recommendations in place. My colleague worked relentlessly and her hard work put in place the most diverse enrichment programmes in the country. Seriously, she worked relentlessly and one working-class boy in the school, who might have otherwise had little interest achieved competition level at sword fencing. That is how diverse the enrichment programme was. My colleague was so committed to her job and worked horrendous hours and as time went on would still be working when I begged her to come for coffee. The following week I was ill and my friend sent me a message telling me. 'Hey gorgeous! 'Do not ever lose your Duffy Sparkle'!

On Tuesday, 1st April 2014 as I ran down to share my day's experiences with my lovely colleague I discovered that she had collapsed on the floor of the school. The following day I discovered she had died. That message is still on an old mobile phone, which I refuse to get rid of

Four days later my gorgeous Father in law died.

In October 2014 I went off ill from work with a virus...... As I lay in an ambulance with sticky pads covering my body the paramedics explained that I was showing all the signs of a heart attack.

How could this happen I was only 48 years old. How could my mind do this to my body?

After 1998, I had never experienced any sort of anxiety or panic, yet I had now found myself in the situation of physical illness. I have read that the biggest regret that people have on their deathbed is that they lived the life expected of them instead of a life true to themselves. I had been so busy living other people's dreams I had lost sight of my own and these words rang in my ears I dusted off the law of attraction books for the next steps forward.

MY HYPNOTHERAPY TRAINING

The incident that occurred in 2014, alongside the way education was going was my wake-up call. The colleague speaking with me about the course was a series of events that led to the start of my training in December 2014. The training that took place with Innervisions School of Clinical Hypnosis taught me about the subconscious mind and how it was always there to protect us. In many ways it put my whole childhood in perspective. The training took place over one full weekend over ten months and was quite intense and becoming a hypnotherapist with Innervisions helped me not only gain an insight into my own life and experiences; It also enabled me to tune into the natural ability that I feel we all have. Some people on the course had attended just for their own personal development. If I had got nothing other than that out of the course I would have still been elated.

The people on the course were three dimensional, they were real people with real lives and I immediately knew that I was in the right place and after completing the free weekend foundation course I signed up for the whole practitioner level course. As the weeks went on I would look forward to the full weekend of learning each and every month. Treatments and methods we learned both theoretically and practically and this put so many things into perspective in my own mind. The other students in the class were friendly and supportive. This was completely different from the academic world in which I had experienced over the last 10 years, which can often be a fiercely competitive environment. When I arrived at the Manchester venue, my tutor Mark Wilson and his wife introduced themselves and were warm and friendly. As the day went on I realised that my friend was not going to attend. This had no impact on my enjoyment and enthusiasm for that first weekend, because clearly, this was my path. I also met some lovely friends and one friend Pauline is still one of my dear friend and we often meet for coffee

Although some of the areas of understanding took a great deal of thinking about, it was different academically, because the learning was brought alive through videos, the informal and friendly nature of my tutor Mark and the practical sessions, which involved working on each other. Early on in the course, we were given MP3's to listen to and this helped. As with any new learning there is always moments of self-doubt. These MP3's were used as self-hypnosis when we needed to improve our confidence in our hypnotherapy and these were really helpful. We were also given access to videos showing hypnotherapy in practice and this was also helpful. By the end of the course, I had two huge folders of support materials including videos, reading material and suggested scripts and the important thing we were encouraged to practice and supported

In addition to all of this, I personally found the training resonated with my life. Firstly, it supported me personally from the perspective of my childhood. The course included different psychological issues which were investigated in depth each month. We learned the science of each issue and an array of social and psychological causes. Treatments and methods we learned both theoretically and practically and this put so many things into perspective in my own mind. My Innervisions hypnotherapy training helped me to understand that as I a five-year-old waiting patiently for my Mother to come back placed me into a world that was neither awake nor asleep. Training also helped me understand that that the subconscious mind is there to protect so understanding this fact it was probably the best place for me to be at that time. I have family members whose experiences from that time have put them much worse position than my own and I am thankful for my protective subconscious.

The training gave me an understanding of how my subconscious had supported my academia. Quite literally without self-hypnosis, I am not sure how I would have gotten through the academic expectations in my journey to being a teacher. Innervisions training gave me an understanding of what I was doing and that was I was utilising the power of my unconscious mind through something that is called a special place and using control room techniques to support my learning. The fact that I pranced about in a mortarboard enabled me to actually experience the situation of graduation which helped me to eventually live out the situation three times in reality through my degree, postgraduate, and masters.

The second thing that I realised midway through the course was that I could achieve and fulfil my life's purpose through other means than working within education. The course included a unit that supported setting up a business and support with marketing including websites and social media. If I am being honest this was an area that I was especially out of my depth with, but the course gave me suggestions and ideas in this area. By the end of the course, I did feel a little nervous about going out on my own. The weekends had been a haven of inspiration and even though I was taking on more work with reading, on top of my full-time teaching; I absolutely loved everything I learned and it seemed to alleviate the pressure. The course quite literally helped me to connected the dots of my life.

Module 9, Inner Child, was especially poignant for me personally it enabled me to dust off the final cobwebs from my childhood and gave me a true and universal experience of how to support the clients that I would work with.

HOW MY LIFE CHANGED AFTER BECOMING A HYPNOTHERAPIST

Since becoming a hypnotherapist I have just become so driven and I believe that I will continue to have a successful hypnotherapy practice. I would eventually like to work within the education system, but this time working from the outside in. Maybe on a freelance basis, as I feel that I have so much to offer education.

My life has changed insofar as I have no regret. I do not regret my initial career in teaching as I know that I have learned so much from my teaching experience. For example, without the experience in education, I would not have fully understood the huge amount of mental health that is occurring within the education system amongst the children and teachers, which I believe cannot be left to continue. The childhood that I experienced or the perception of that childhood has given me a fantastic grounding to understand that past trauma can creep up on you even when you least expect it.

In addition to this I am so glad that I experienced hypnotherapy in 1998, because it allowed me to see hypnotherapy from a different perspective (from the client's perspective) Having those feelings of not understanding what hypnotherapy was and then actually experiencing the life-changing benefits is something that I was lucky enough to benefit from. Ironically, even though I told people how wonderful hypnotherapy was for over 18 years, I never dreamed of utilising it as a career. During the 18 years after 1998 and whilst training and working in teaching, I read books on psychology and therapy sessions just for fun. Therefore, reading and research to support clients is something that I am inspired to do.

The second thing that I realised midway through the course was that I could achieve and fulfil my life's purpose through alternative means other than working within education. The course included a unit that supported setting up a business and marketing including websites and social media. If I am being honest this was an area that I was especially out of my depth with, but the course gave me suggestions and ideas in this area. By the end of the course, I did feel a little nervous about going out on my own. The weekends had been a haven and inspiration and even though I was taking on more work with reading, on top of my full-time teaching. I absolutely loved everything I learned and it seemed to alleviate the pressure I felt.

CLIENT SUCCESS STORY ONE

The client success story that stays with me after completing my training as a hypnotherapist involved a set of unfortunate events. Yet it is something that was almost a harsh reminder that I needed to move forward with my journey

On the 2nd April 2017, I decided to attend a Mental Health First Aid course run by Innervisions School of Clinical Hypnosis trainer Val Goff, who had a background working in mental health and found the course extremely disturbing, but elements of the course also resonated with what I was witnessing in education. A few weeks later on 29th April 2017, I witness and gained an understanding into the power of EFT and how it had been particularly successful with Post-traumatic stress disorder with soldiers who had experienced harrowing experiences. Little was I to know how powerful the training I had received could be.

On the Wednesday`10th May I woke to feel particularly sick with horrific headaches and phoned in work sick taking myself to bed. Later on that day around 5.00 pm an ex work colleague told me about an incident that had occurred in school.

A teenager was fighting for life after suffering serious head injuries when he plunged from a balcony at a school.

The 18-year-old boy was left in a serious condition after falling inside the school.

The following day as I went into school and I was immediately inspired by the new Head Teacher who had just started at the school, yet handled the incident well. As lots of students were rushing around getting ready for registration a colleague informed me how the student had jumped from the second floor and how, even though the Head Teacher had handled the incident well, many students witnessed it and were traumatised by the incident.

In the past, I had experienced some different emotive incidents over the years and I had been left feeling helpless and out of control, but here I was experiencing this particular incident I had just completed a mental health first aid course, and a course in EFT which supported post-traumatic syndrome and I also had my hypnotherapy training. By Friday many of the sixth form students and staff who had witnessed the incident were feeling overwhelmed. After the incident and the fact that we only had a small group of 'A' level students, around 30 students per year, students had been close to each other and many of them felt guilt in not noticing any warning signs to the trauma.

The Head Teacher at the school supported the school by getting outside agencies in, but they were overwhelmed and not always available. At 3.00pm I was asked by the head of the sixth form if I was able to support a student who was experiencing extreme trauma after the incident.

The staff were fearful of sending her home amidst fears of suicide and it was so humbling to be able to support the student. It was humbling that I was able to support her using the EFT techniques. The thing was I was not the all-powerful one, I would hate that. What in fact was happening was I was using a technique that I had learned to help to empower the students to utilise their own power to deal with the trauma they had experienced.

Another aspect of the incident was that unfortunately, this incident was in the middle of the student's A-level exams. After I supported the student with her trauma, within days I had a queue of students and staff at my door asking if they could see me rather than the outside agencies that had been brought in. It was so inspiring for me as a therapist in building my confidence. Whilst teaching I guess I had created good rapport with the students and staff due to the fact that they had got to know me. The school where happy for me to conduct therapies between teaching. Even though I felt exhausted, I have never felt so useful in being able to support these young people.

One student who had witnessed the incident was a lovely young lady I had taught for seven year. It was so upsetting to discover that she was struggling to focus on exams after the incident.

After finishing her GCSE's with me she had gone on to study at A-level. She was a working class girl with aspirations to achieve and worked a part-time job in the school cleaning. Each and every evening after school she would come after school and talk to me about her hopes and dreams. Therefore, when she came to me so upset about the fact that she was struggling with her Art 'A' level it perturbed me. She trusted me and explained that she felt unable to complete her Art exam, even though I knew she had completed so much research and clearly had the potential to achieve. The incident had resulted in a creative blockage and she was concerned.

Obviously, her needs were at the forefront of in my mind and when she came to me it was a no-brainer. I felt so blessed that I was able to trust me and I was able to support her and after the session which included EFT and hypnotherapy. After the exam she came skipping to me asking me to look at what she had achieved. The exam that she had completed was creative and even before actually having the work marked, she knew that she had done well and was so proud of her artistic efforts.

After the two incidents, the queues at my door were soon brought to the attention of other people who were responsible for the health and wellbeing of students and staff within the school. After a few days, I received emails that portrayed concerns over my wellbeing. I explained via email that I had the full support of Innervisions who were extremely supportive in this area. After a couple of days, I was advised in the most polite emails that my services were no longer needed.

That is the public sector you see. Everything is about ticking a particular box that is required and the human factor seems to have disappeared.

Nevertheless, the event was totally inspiring, this and other events during that time had inspired me to understand that I had already decided that the only way to make the difference that I wanted to make in education and with young people was from the outside in. Completing my course in hypnotherapy, mental health, EFT and Law of Attraction had enabled me to take the rose coloured glasses off and allowed me to visualise the vibrant colours of reality.

CLIENT SUCCESS STORY TWO

The other client story that stays with me was my first smoker. She had smoked for over 30 years and whilst I went through the preamble beforehand and then the hypnotherapy session I awaited her dropping the cigarette from her hand. Initially, she hesitated, but then dropped the cigarette. She is still a none smoker and I am still amazed by the power of the mind. In fact, even now after completing hypnotherapy sessions I am in awe when experiencing each and every session and the power of the mind and the strength and character of the people I have worked with.

MY HYPNOTHERAPY PRACTICE

Butterfly Effect Transformation is my hypnotherapy practice, which is based in Audenshaw near Ashton –under-Lyne. Initially, after finishing and qualifying as a hypnotherapist with Innervisions School of Clinical Hypnosis, I set the practice up in my own name. However, things really started to get moving once I attended the law of attraction course run by Brian Glenn, who is the principal of Innervisions School of Clinical Hypnosis and I would argue that this enabled me to start calving the hypnotherapy practice of my dreams. As I mentioned previously I had always been inspired by the law of attraction and when I saw the course I felt that it would be a great way to re-inspire me to get on with moving my life forward and go over what I had read about in the book 'The Secret', many years before. However, I was totally surprised when I attended the course as Brian's course included a whole new slant on the law of attraction, which investigated the science behind the law of attraction.

Within weeks of attending the course, my mind was working overtime and I had come up with the name *'Butterfly Effect Transformation'* for my business. In addition to this, I loved the slogan: change one thing, change everything. The name and slogan come from the scientific theory that a single occurrence, no matter how small, can change the course of the whole universe forever. I love this idea and it resonates with me when I am completing therapies. It also helps me as I utilise it when working towards my own dreams.

Sometimes with anything in life, whether that be illness, goals or business, it is difficult to move forward due to being overwhelmed. My friend who died had shared the dreams for her book with me with deep emotion, but although she could explain to me some of the finer details she had never started the book. She had lived her life for other people and not fulfilled her own dreams to write her book and that still stays with me.

Therefore, I made sure that with everything I have done around my business I have broken it down, chunked it up, but always move forward. An example of using this was when initially got the idea for my business name and was so excited to get going on with driving my business forward. My son was in Hong Kong and I had no idea how to set up websites, social media or other things. However, I utilised my own slogan and one step at a time (with a lot of swearing) was able to slowly work my way through designing my own website. Granted it took some weeks, but each and every slow, tiny step moved me forward.

Some people reading this might think it is not a big deal, but remember I still work and have a family; these changes stop me from remaining stagnant and help move my business forward. Currently, I have to work to fund my business and thankfully as I finish at 4 pm I am able to see clients after work and during holidays. This will change as next year I have a property being built with, which also includes a separate hypnotherapy clinic. It is hard work at the moment, but I am totally motivated by the journey I am on and cannot wait to see where I will be next year. The other message I use to inspire clients is 'be the change you want to see' and I also try to live by this slogan. I drive myself forward as and still use self-hypnosis to motivate myself whilst awaiting the building of my business.

My business and clients motivate me and recently the local homeless charities have contacted me to ask me to give inspirational talks on the types of thing I do through my business to support the homeless. I felt so privileged. This is extra work, but I love this sort of thing. The ladies running three of the charities are ladies that have become disillusioned with working in the NHS and one had become disillusioned as a noise abatement officer with not being able to support the homeless. Seriously, when I met these inspirational ladies I felt that I was right where I needed to be. My friend (who I met on the course) always says after coffee… 'Gaynor you are my inspiration'. However, recently she has become my inspiration as she has just landed a hypnotherapy post with the NHS

During my hypnotherapy training, I had experienced a fear of public speaking, ridiculous I know because I teach teenagers. However, seriously I had an anxiety about speaking in front of other adults, I was so nervous. After experiencing hypnotherapy for this, I am so excited to speak in front of these charities to spread the word about how hypnotherapy can have a huge impact on the lives of people who approach these charities.

Today whilst writing, I opened up my emails to find that I have gained a qualification for the top three businesses in Tameside. It feels so exciting and I now truly know that I am on a path to make changes that will make me feel that getting up in a morning and starting work is inspirational, motivational and life-changing. This is only a local award, but I know it is one of many. As I continue to dream, work hard and stay focused I know that I will: 'be the change that I want to see'.

Innervisions School of Clinical Hypnosis support has always been a click away as we are given supervision and support personally and through an online support website where an array of supportive and experienced psychotherapists, mental health professionals, and hypnotherapists with a wealth of experience. Courses are run by some of the most experienced people and professionals and as many of my clients were suffering from a whole host of mental health issues I signed up for a course with the Mental health professional Val Goff. The Mental Health First Aid course was so informative and relayed the issues within mental health that I myself had seen in education when working with teaching staff and children. These have also been witnessed within the courts and this highlight the crisis around mental health within wider society. A month later and with the issues of mental health evident within my clients I signed up for the EFT course. The same week I also signed up for the Law of Attraction course, and if I am being honest I did not imagine it would give me any more information than I already knew. I could not have been more wrong and at the time could not have known the impact that all three courses would have.

Even after completing the hypnotherapy course I had not met Brian Glenn as he now lives in Spain and semi-retired, but has competent tutors teaching his courses in various locations around the U.K. The first course I attended was an EFT course and we were given research evidence of how EFT was one of the best types of therapies being utilised within the armed forces to support post-traumatic syndrome. We were also taught how to entwine this into our hypnotherapy.

Brian also ran a law of attraction course and when he introduced himself to the class I was amazed to hear a quick overview of his story. He like me, had experienced a colourful childhood and career and had come from a working-class family, but had turned his childhood struggles around in an effort to inspire and make a difference to at least a million people. Brian was three dimensional and full of character and his unique take on the law of attraction included the science around it and it blew my mind. During practice sessions I was put into hypnosis by a fellow student and had the most inspirational vision to date. This time I had an end point I saw myself as a successful business women, not necessarily linked to education, just successful in my own right. The image was absolutely inspirational and I have held onto that image as a way to drive my business forward and was a motivating factor in my butterfly motif and logo.

As she lights the next match, she sees a vision of herself through her subconscious, the only thing to have treated her with love and kindness all through her life. To keep the vision of herself alive for as long as she can, the girl lights the entire bundle of matches at once and as she holds the spent matchsticks within her hands, she feels a burning and she opens her hands and a beautiful blue butterfly emerges from her hands.

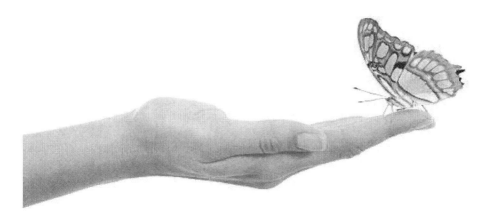

Next year my business premises will be built and within two years I will have a full-time business and will impact education from the outside in. How do I know this? - Because I saw it and I felt it!

Thank you Innervisions School of Clinical Hypnosis.

CONTACT DETAILS:

Name: Gaynor Marie Duffy
Telephone: (07443) 424293
Email: gaynor@betransformation.com
Website: www.betransformation.com
Facebook: https://www.facebook.com/gaynor.duffy

PETER WALL: INNERLIGHT HYPNOSIS

BEFORE BECOMING A HYPNOTHERAPIST

If I could turn the clock back to the late 1970's and hear someone say 'Peter, one day you will become a Clinical Hypnotherapist and Past Life Regressionist' I would have laughed my socks off! Yet that is exactly where and what I am today here in 2017. I have now been a qualified Hypnotherapist for over 15 years and the reason for that happening? Well it was like this.

When I was a young lad wherever possible I would love to watch the old black and white movies where actors dressed in top hats, black cloaks and it seemed always had a long moustache. The impression that their eyes would light up and there would always be a demure lady who would appear to be put into some form of a trance, would fascinate me. Actors such as Lon Chaney, John Barrymore and Bella Lougsi would appear to hypnotize people into a trance and make them do their bidding! How could this work? I would often try waving my grandfather's pocket watch in front of my siblings to make them act silly – but that one never seemed to work for me!

I also had a deep fascination for Magic and how the mind could be tricked into believing that a coin for example could suddenly disappear from the magician's hand! I would even ask my parents to buy me the magic box of tricks for my birthday or as a Christmas gift, just to see how and learn how these types of tricks could work for myself.

On entering into the work place at the age of 15, I found it difficult to maintain a job that would hold my attention and interest for any great length of time. I became a Class 2 Welder, then went onto qualify as a City and Guilds Bricklayer, then onto selling Double Glazing, to even setting up my own Party Plan business selling bedding.

You will see by reading from just these few listings that I soon became bored and restless and seemed to always be looking for that something that would truly keep me occupied and interested. No job it would appear could give me that job satisfaction that I was constantly looking for and so much to the exasperation of my wife we decided to change roles.

I became house husband and she the "bread winner". This also gave me the opportunity in what had been initially a hobby to work with and being creative with stained glass. During some of my free time when the children were at school, I began to dabble in making various items such as Glass Vases and Mirrors and began selling them at various craft fairs and events close to home.

It was whilst I was attending a Craft fair a gentleman approached me and asked if I could make a Pyramid in Glass for his wife to cleanse and re-energies her crystals. I will admit I was bemused by this request, but never wanting to turn down a challenge I agreed. After much research on the dimensions and history surrounding the pyramids – in particular the pyramids at Giza in Egypt the pyramid was duly prepared and low and behold I had lost the gentleman's details!

A colleague whom I had met at one of the Craft fairs I attended, told me about an event which was being held at Ilkley and thought it may be worth my while to take my pyramids along to this event. This was not the usual type of Craft Fair I would normally attend but was known as a Well Being Event but me being me thought I would give anything a try. So off I went. This turned out in 1998 to be my very first Mind Body and Spirit exhibition and where I became known as 'Pyramids by Pierre'.

MY HYPNOTHERAPY TRAINING

It was during one of the events held in Ilkley in 2001, I met Brian Glenn of Innversions School of Clinical Hypnosis and it was at this point my life and direction where about to completely change.

As I have mentioned previously Hypnosis (albeit mostly stage Hypnosis) had always fascinated me. So when on a short break during the show and I went for a walkabout I spotted Brian's stand, where there was an Hypnotic Spiral and this drew me into a conversation between the two of us.

I soon learnt from him that there was far more to just the "fun side" to Hypnosis and that it could be taken to a more professional clinical basis to help people in many ways and this intrigued me even more. After my chat with Brian I took home some of the literature about his school, Innervisons and on how to become a Clinical Hypnotherapist.
It did not take me long to make up my mind that this was something I would like to do. All that earlier fascination now started to make sense. By the year 2002 I had qualified and became a member of the National Council of Psychotherapy. I initially worked with my clients using a variety of alternative therapy premises available in and around the Barnsley Area which is where I am based.

Each day was different, albeit perhaps I met and dealt with people with similar issues where Hypnotherapy could assist and help but each client was an individual and my focus was solely on helping them to overcome whatever their issue(s) may have been. No more boredom or loss of interest – I had found my personal goal! So much so that by 2007 I had the opportunity to open my own Hypnotherapy clinic in the village of Cawthorne and remained there until April 2016.

HOW MY LIFE CHANGED AFTER BECOMING A HYPNOTHERAPIST

Since that first encounter all those years ago in Ilkley with Brian, I have never once felt the need to look back or think what am I doing here as I had in all my other previous jobs. On the contrary I have had the opportunity to work and help people from all walks of life during my years as a Hypnotherapist.

Hypnotherapy has also helped me personally. There was no one more timid when it came to Public Speaking and I had very little self-esteem so by using self-hypnosis this put me in good stead in my career and allowed me to encourage others to be the same.

There has been no greater feeling for me personally to have a client walk into my therapy room looking and feeling dull, dejected and with no self-esteem. To see them leave looking happy, smiling and more positive.

CLIENT SUCCESS STORY ONE

Past Life Regression became my forte and I was highly delighted to be invited to appear on the BBC's Big Question with Nicky Campbell on the chosen subject "Have we lived before?" I will admit I was extremely nervous but at the same time fascinated by listening to the various arguments for those who said they believed it to be true and those who said it could not be! Till it came to my turn!!

I had asked if one of my clients whom I had regressed a few months previously could join me and who had actually taken the time out to research the details we had gleaned during her regression.

She was known as Tamar Scot in this Past Life Regression. On searching and looking up various records this unusual name was found and concurred with the exact location of the address she had given me during her regression and also she was found to be registered at the time she had referred to on the census of the year in question. Further research showed her place of birth, where she had worked. She even obtained a copy of her marriage certificate during her research and brought this along as proof to the programme.

CLIENT SUCCESS STORY TWO

Another client whom I regressed informed me whilst in hypnosis, that he was a Native American Indian. I asked him if he would tell me what tribe he belonged to and could he speak to me in his native tongue. I will be honest when he said he was Inuit, I had no idea. Sioux, Cheyenne and one or two other tribes I would have easily recognised but this left me somewhat bewildered. We continued into the regression where he spoke quite fluently in his native language. Further research using the help of a colleague who was into languages at the time, established he had in fact been telling the women of the village to get cracking as winter was coming and they were not doing their job correctly in preparing the skins and food for the coming months!! I will mention at this point my client was one of the softest characters in this life you could ever meet and would not say 'boo to a goose'! So to hear this strong and determined voice left all three of us quite amused. We also discovered that the Inuit where also known as Eskimos in today's terminology.

CLIENT SUCCESS STORY THREE

It doesn't surprise me when a client is disappointed to learn that they were merely a farmer's wife, a candlestick maker or fisherman. Not a King, or a Princess which they had fanciful whished for when being regressed but just good old ordinary folk of which there are many and only a few from nobility!

Such one occasion during one of the MBS events that comes to mind was a lady who came to see me for regression. This lady was very well attired and her hair had been immaculately done. She held a fascination about Past Lives and during my preamble with her found out she believed she had been a person of some nobility in a past life. The regression was going well, when she started to scratch at her head rather vigorously and started to rub her nose as if to eliminate an odour. It turned out she was the daughter of a pig farmer in 1700's, lived in very poor conditions and had fleas!! We concluded the regression and off she went. A few hours later she returned and I thought something was wrong. She informed me that the regression had left her with the understanding of why since a small child she had always collected pigs, be it pictures, ornaments and the like. I in turn thanked her for letting me know but I will admit I did not have the heart to tell her that the immaculate hair do was somewhat dishevelled! But I guess she found that out when she got home!

I will admit when I was first asked if I offered Past Life Regression I viewed it with some scepticism. At the beginning of my career I felt Hypnotherapy was the main tool for Stop Smoking, Weight Loss and overcoming Fears and Phobias etc., but since working with many clients who have asked for exploratory Past Life Regression and then for the client to research that information that has been given turns out to be factual, then I am now personally of the firm belief, that there is more to this mere mortal coil in which we all reside!

MY HYPNOTHERAPY PRACTICE

There is and can be no greater satisfaction in seeing a client change their mind set. See them loose weight or stop smoking or be finally able to go on that aircraft that will allow them to have the holiday of a lifetime which they believed for many years would never happen.

Although I no longer have Cawthorne Hypnotherapy clinic I still continue to work as Innerlight Hypnosis with clients within their own homes or a small therapy room I have the use of in premises near to me. And I continue to attend a variety of Mind Body and Well Being events around the U.K.

My work as a Clinical Hypnotherapist still keeps me occupied and it never bores me. It has given me personally a great sense of achievement and has only come about since that first encounter with Brian Glenn back in 2001. To that person I say a BIG thank you.

I had planned to 'retire' but I have come to realise there is no such thing and continue to work with clients now in their own homes and have a therapy room in Doncaster. Although perhaps working on a more semi-retired basis. While ever I am able to help my clients I will continue to do so.

There are so many myths and misunderstandings about Hypnosis, but it is an amazing therapy to help and overcome so many things, such as fears and phobias which may come in many forms and these are invariably started in early years. But, by using Hypnotherapy, which has been around for hundreds of years, these can be overcome after just one or two sessions.

The use of Hypnotherapy to help with Public Speaking and to become more self-confident is now becoming more widespread. Of course there are the usual matters such as Stop Smoking and Weight Control where Hypnotherapy has become more predominately used over the past decade, especially with the onset of the Virtual Gastric Band method for weight control for clients who are classed as morbidly obese.

I have also become well known for my work with Past Lives and this is now one of my key areas where I use Hypnosis to enable clients to explore their past lives in a safe, secure and enjoyable way. I am also now accredited by the NCP to teach Past Life Regression to other Professionals who deal with the General Public and these workshops are growing in popularity.

Since my very first event in Ilkley all those years ago, I have attended numerous MBS and Well Being events the length and breadth of the country and worked abroad in Germany, Jersey and Spain.

I am particularly proud to have been one of the first exhibitors to join Liz Clark and Ian Timothy of Lizian Well Being Events at the start of their MBS Events journey some four years ago, and look forward to continue to support them for the foreseeable future at all their future events, including Lincoln, Cheltenham, Newark and Nottingham to promote Hypnotherapy, my Past life Regression Teaching and The Peter Wall Way to Self Help Cd's at these events.

CONTACT DETAILS:

Name: Peter Wall
Telephone: (07973) 736511
Email: peter.wall@live.co.uk
Website: www.innerlight-hypnosis.com
Facebook: www.facebook.com/peter.wall.54584

STEVEN SMITH: SCS HYPNOSIS

BEFORE BECOMING A HYPNOTHERAPIST

My primary focus over the years has always been on my wonderful children, Amelia, Shane, and Owen. After the birth of my daughter I chose to be a stay at home parent and as any stay at home parent knows there are many challenges to face. It's taxing on the mind and the body. Before becoming a stay at home parent, I had previously worked in retail, sales, call centres, offices, and food, but never felt satisfied by this type of work. I always felt that there was something I was missing, I just didn't know what.

MY HYPNOTHERAPY TRAINING

In my search to find what I was missing and improve my life and that of my families, I came across hypnosis. At first, it seemed a bit mystical and strange, but the more I researched it, the more mesmerized by the subject and the power of the subconscious mind has over us.

Once I had gained an interested in the field of hypnosis and its power to help change, I knew it was time to home my skills and expand my knowledge on the human mind and how to use hypnosis to resolve unwanted issues. At this point, I began searching for a training school that offered the best course and met my needs. I came across a post on my Facebook newsfeed offering a free weekends training. Although I was rather dubious and sceptical, I decided to apply and attended the weekend with an open mind. After ten months of intensive training with Innervisions School of Clinical Hypnosis, I finally qualified in October 2016, and since then never looked back.

HOW MY LIFE CHANGED AFTER BECOMING A HYPNOTHERAPIST

Hypnotherapy has changed my life in many ways. For some people, they train to change their career, or train because they want to help people, and some others train to improve the quality of their own life. For me, it was all these and more. I have seen the benefits of hypnosis and decided to learn because it had, and continues to have such a life-changing effect. I have listed a few of the main ways becoming a hypnotherapist has changed my life, otherwise, I would be writing a book just on how much it has improved my life:

- ✓ Job satisfaction. Nothing else comes remotely close. When I help a client and they say, "Thank you, you have changed my life," it feels so much better than achieving any sales target for an employer I've ever worked for.

- ✓ I have developed a massive pride in what I do. To help someone to get over their obstacle or to help them make a new start, or change their outlook from negative to positive, you will feel proud of what you and they have achieved, and rightly so.

✓ Being self-employed allows me to make all the decisions and work around my family's needs, this gives me a real sense of freedom. There is no one telling me what to do, I can charge what I like, work when I like and specialise in certain areas of interest such as Self-esteem and confidence.

✓ I can work from home, from a Therapy Centre, outdoors or even visit my clients. I'm not tied down to the same four walls like previous office job and retail work. Making life fun and ever-changing.

✓ Flexible working hours. I work as often as I wish, when I wish. If I have a family emergency or not feeling up to it I can choose to work or not, I have no one to report.

✓ Constant self-improvement. The skills I have learnt have helped me in every aspect of my life, from managing stress to stopping personal bad habits, and being motivated to live a healthier lifestyle.

And of course, there's that add bonus of building your own business and seeing your hard work pay off, bring with it a sense of joy and satisfaction.

Qualifying in clinical hypnosis, really allowed me to home my skills and help more people than I ever be I could.

CLIENT SUCCESS STORY ONE

An example of these skills in use was when I was helping a 42 year old gent with a sleeping disorder. For over a year he was unable to stay asleep, suffering from sleep jerks, getting only an hour or so at a time. This was resulting in him being unable to go to work, unable to socialise, losing confidence within himself and thinking that this was going to be his life.

After a few weekly sessions and being taught self-hypnosis techniques, we had addressed the reason for his sleep jerk and his sleep had begun to improve, reaching about five hours solid sleep per night. This five hours of sleep had already began to have a massive impact on his energy levels. He had once again started feeling more confident about himself, started socialising with friends and decided to follow his dreams of starting his own business. Something he had been putting off and was one of the reasons he wasn't sleeping, as his subconscious was struggling to work out what his true desire was, and with the help of hypnosis, he managed to resolve it and improve his quality of life.

CLIENT SUCCESS STORY TWO

Another time that these skills were a massive help was when I had the pleasure of working with a 31-year-old lady who decided to have hypnotherapy to help her reduce weight. As a licenced hypnoslimmer consultant, I used the renowned hypnoslimmer weight control system with this lady who had struggled with her weight for many years and had tried every diet she could find. She didn't have any confidence in herself and this was a real problem for her. She was also concerned about passing this fear on to her children. This lady's weight had reached over 16 stone which for her height of 5ft 5 was getting very close to being morbidly obese. She really couldn't see how life could change for her and was almost at the point of accepting that's how her life would be from then on. After a four week weight reduction program, she had already reduced three dress sizes, giving her more confidence and feeling healthier. Three months after treatment she continued to reduce and her Life has completely changed. She has become more and more confident within herself. She is happy and enjoying buying new clothes in a size 10 rather than a size 22. She has completely turned her life around and loving it, all that from addressing her association with food and resetting her natural hunger cycle.

www.hypnoslimmer.eu

MY LIFE AS A CLINICAL HYPNOTHERAPIST

Well, as I've mentioned before there is nothing that comes close, when it comes to job reward and satisfaction. Whether you are helping a smoker to quit smoking overnight, helping someone release a phobia or a fear that has affected their quality of life for years, helping somebody reach new performance highs, or one of hundred different things that hypnosis helps facilitate change, it always feels good.

It never becomes routine as you are always dealing with people, and we are all unique and have unique challenges in our lives. So just imagine, you were suddenly able to solve an issue that has been the cause of a client's so pain for months, even years, and they have got to the point that they believe that there current situation is the end of the line and that they just have to make the best of a bad situation, then you suddenly help them to make a change, even a small change. You help them make this change, and it can be so profound, so dramatic that they are now seeing their issue in a whole new light and realising that it wasn't really that bad in the first place. They begin to smile again, begin enjoying life again. How great would that feel? For me it fills me with a sense of pride and joy, knowing that not only have I helped someone to achieve something wonderful but that my hard work and dedication has paid off.

The one thing that can seem a little strange when you begin practising is getting your client into hypnosis, to have them seem completely uninterested in anything that you have to say or do, and you can feel like you're just talking to yourself. But you get used that after a while, especially as you begin to gain confidence from the hard evidence that your work is producing beneficial and life-changing results. Your clients will continually tell you about their improvements and that they feel much better.

The truly great thing about being a hypnotherapist is that you can bring every resource that you possess into your therapy. Hypnotherapists come from all walks of life. In my class there was a shop assistant, holistic therapist, builder, ballroom dancer, housewife/househusband (like myself), those recently made redundant, the unemployed, anyone who fancies a change of career. All you have to do is study and put in the effort, and even allow yourself to question some long-held beliefs about you and grow; it can turn out to be best career choice that you have ever made.

MY HYPNOTHERAPY PRACTICE

Since qualifying and starting full-time from day one as a full-time hypnotherapist, I have built up a successful and steady practice here in Darton, Barnsley, with a mobile service also available to those in the Wakefield and South Leeds area. Working from Activ-Health Sports Therapy clinic in Darton also allows me to offer all hypnotherapy and EFT treatments including Hypnosis Law of Attraction to all who wish to experience hypnosis for specific goal. Specialising in Self-esteem, confidence and fitness, which I believe to be the three corner stones to a happy healthy mind and body.

I am fortunate to have found and trained with Innervisions School of Clinical Hypnosis, who are one of the UK's top training providers in clinical hypnosis, and I am happy to play a role in Brian Glenn's lifetime quest to help one million people. This has allowed me to help so many people find their true-self so that they can now live the life they have always dreamed of, and not the one that has been forced on them from out influences.

Thank you for reading my contribution to this book. Wishing you well and all the best for your future.

CONTACT DETAILS:

Name:	Steven Smith
Telephone:	(07432) 464960
Email:	info@scshypnosis.com
Website:	www.scshypnosis.com
Facebook:	www.facebook.com/scshypnosis

LES ROBERTS: LES ROBERTS HYPNOTHERAPY and NLP

BEFORE BECOMING A HYPNOTHERAPIST

On reflection, I have always enjoyed helping others. As a child, I used to visit the local retirement home and read stories to the residents, brush their hair and paint their nails. I helped with our elderly neighbours, babysat for family friends and had a very happy childhood.

After leaving college with bilingual secretarial qualifications, I had a few jobs here and there. However, nothing meant much. I looked on these jobs as just that. Turn up, work, go home. A job to bring in a regular wage, money to spend on whatever I wanted to spend it on. I never settled in one job longer than a few years, never really achieving much. After having three children, I decided I needed to do something more with my life. So in 2003 I secured a post within the NHS, working as part of an Integrated Therapy Team, consisting of Occupational Therapists, Physiotherapists and Speech and Language Therapists. For over 10 years I worked with children 0-19, in Special Schools and throughout the community. I gained knowledge in behaviours, how perceptions can become beliefs and sometimes hold a person back from achieving their potential. I learned how vitally important it is to treat the individual not the ailment or diagnosis. The main part of my role was teaching children different methods of communication, including sign language and electronic devices, helping with mobility, specialist seating, splinting, demonstrating fine motor skill movements and observing Carers and Families carrying out therapy programmes to increase continuity. My day was never the same and very busy!! Although I was happy and enjoyed my job, I never felt completely fulfilled. Something was missing. I hadn't a clue what this was. In search of finding out what I really was missing, I enrolled in a Child Psychology course as a distance learner. Wow! It was an eye opener! Behaviours! Just what I was searching for! This was the beginning of my studies again. I completed it within 3 months, even though it was a 12-month course. Although it gave me a greater insight into behaviours, it didn't really fill the gap and I grew restless again. After a disastrous interview for a higher band, I informed my seniors my intentions to leave as I felt the need to start spreading my wings a little further. I was upset and angry that even after over 10 years working in the same team, whether I was successful or not for a similar yet higher post, depended on how I answered the questions during the interview. My Manager realised how this had affected me and offered to fund a course as a way of placating me to stay.

I booked myself onto an NLP Foundation Course. This course was 45 miles away from home. I had to attend both Saturday and Sunday. This meant driving on a very busy motorway there and back twice. I was terrified of motorway slip roads, however determined to conquer my fear. And that's exactly what I did. A Practitioner in NLP, who was assisting on the course, noticed how unsettled I was and offered to help me. She installed an anchor for me to overcome my fear of motorway slip roads. The beginning of my wonderful journey of self-change began there and then. I completed the course and immediately enrolled to become a Practitioner.

I self-funded my Practitioner Course in NLP and continued to study for other qualifications. Within a few years I had qualified in Child Psychology, as an NLP Practitioner, Reiki Practitioner, Integral Eye Movement Therapist and EFT Practitioner. All these qualifications! What was I supposed to do with them? Where do I begin? Fate intervened and in September 2014 I lost my job. I registered with Agencies and became a locum for NHS services, whilst completing my studies.

MY HYPNOTHERAPY TRAINING

I had noticed the advertisement for Innervisions School of Clinical Hypnosis a few times on Facebook. A free weekend? No strings attached? No obligation? No hard sell? Although I was interested, I considered the cost implications outweighed my need for further education/courses. A few months later, the advertisement popped up again and I responded. The free weekend was exactly that. An incredibly interesting insight into the fantastic workings and powerful methodologies of Hypnotherapy. This was my true "lightbulb" moment. This course and qualification is most probably the path I was subconsciously looking for. It turned out it most definitely was.

I enrolled on the full course. Having the option to pay monthly fell perfectly with my financial situation. I even booked into the hotel for each weekend of the course, having a bit of me time away from home. There was a variety of skill mix in our small group, from Insurance Clerks, Nurse, Estate Agent, Teaching Assistant, Beautician to Counsellor. Our tutor, Mark was amazing. So knowledgeable, so organised, patient, empathic.

The weekends on the course went by so quickly. Each module was delivered professionally and met our needs. Mark had time for every one of us, taking an interest in our lives as well as answering any questions we may have pertaining to the course. Mark encouraged us to believe in ourselves, strengthening our weaknesses and building on our strengths.

Every weekend we studied different modules, all handouts and folders were included in the cost of the course. The camaraderie within the group was amazing. Along with Mark's excellent tutorials, videos, and opportunities to practice our new-found art, the course was extremely enjoyable and very informative. My toolbox was becoming healthy and overflowed with useful and important tools to guide and help others. By the end of the course, I felt a great accomplishment. Not only did the course teach me how to be a professional Clinical Hypnotherapist, it also helped me to become a better person, to be more positive in life and given me a totally new direction. One I'm loving and enjoying!! I am proud to have studied with Innervisions. They have become my extended family and we all do our best to support each other. After qualification, you are not left out there alone and wondering what to do next. You become a part of an ever-increasing family of fellow Hypnotherapists. Each one unique, yet the same!

HOW MY LIFE CHANGED AFTER BECOMING A HYPNOTHERAPIST

Life as a Hypnotherapist can be tough sometimes, however, I wouldn't change my decision. I'm loving my journey, I feel almost complete. The highs, like when I help someone to alter their outlook on life and make dramatic changes, completely outweigh the lows. The buzz I get when my clients make those positive breakthroughs is euphoric. This feeling has not gone away; every client brings something different to my clinic, a new challenge, a new opportunity to. I enjoy meeting people, talking and helping. Each client comes through my door, wanting to change for the better, putting their trust in me. Overall, it is rewarding and very satisfying. Helping people is paramount to my success. I'm determined to be successful and to run a professional business, establishing myself as a reputable Therapist.

Have I helped my family at all using Hypnotherapy? Of course! They are my 'guinea pigs'. My daughter has overcome her fear of flying and now holds a job working abroad. My son experienced Past Life Regression and was overwhelmed at who he found out he was. My grandsons both really love relaxing using visualisation and imagination with hypnotherapy. They imagine they are jumping from island to island, playing with their favourite characters. My husband has watched me at work with my family, however has not experienced hypnotherapy yet. Should you asked him though, he'd tell you I have hypnotised him in one form or other. Suddenly, he feels happy to carry out DIY in our garden and home plus appears to always be in the kitchen, washing the pots!! The power of suggestion at its best!!!

CLIENT SUCCESS STORY ONE

One of my very first and extremely memorable Hypnotherapy clients was a lovely gentleman who came to see me saying he had a phobia of needles. His wish was to overcome this phobia as he was diabetic and had been informed he may need to self-administer insulin via needle. He had been in a traffic accident a few years ago, resulting in walking with crutches and taking opiates daily for his pain. His sugar levels were becoming out of control and his pain was increasing. He wasn't sleeping very well and his libido was very low. He was stressing over his lack of intimacy with his young wife and was worried she may leave him. I asked him how he came to have his phobia of needles. He replied he was told this by a nurse when he went for a blood test as he became agitated and nervous when she was drawing blood from him.

My usual practice is to ask my clients to compete an intake form. This consists of important information, asking relevant questions appertaining to their needs, likes, dislikes etc. He came to see me 3 times in total. Not only did we explore his fear of needles (no phobia), we also worked on improving his sleeping pattern and reducing his pain. What happen then for him was a massive shift in his lifestyle. By reducing his pain, he was sleeping better and not taking as much pain relief medication. This led to him not getting up in the middle of the night and eating sweet treats out of the fridge, hence his blood sugars were more stable. As he was sleeping better, he felt overall much calmer and less stressed. His relationship with his wife improved massively, resulting in a gorgeous baby boy!! If anyone is my biggest advocate that I can help, it's him.

CLIENT SUCCESS STORY TWO

Another gentleman came to see me for his insecurities. His view on life was a very pessimistic one. He was afraid to fly, of heights, he was adamant he was depressed all the time. He believed if anything good happened to him, it would be taken away in one form or other. We worked on his confidence initially, along with his self-belief and self-esteem. Each time he came through my door, I could see the positive changes in him. His last visit, we worked on his issue with heights. I received a telephone call from his wife a few weeks later. He'd been to Florida, on a plane (!!) and even went on some high rides with his family!! Wow!!

One of my proudest achievements to date is being invited to talk at a public event. I was approached on social media and asked if I would like to speak about my passion for hypnotherapy and NLP. I spoke for 20 minutes on neuro pathways and neuroplasticity. To share a stage with established professionals was exciting yet a touch daunting. After my first standing ovation, I was completely overwhelmed and so proud of myself. I've been asked to return once more to speak again.

I have spoken on 2 radio stations, one for smoking cessation and the other about hypnotherapy in general. I have been invited back to speak further about hypnotherapy, the workings of the brain and the power of suggestion.

I attend Mind Body and Soul events to network, build and establish my company, occasionally speaking to audiences on topics I am passionate about.

I run Ladies' Wellbeing Courses, teaching ladies to love themselves, use positive affirmations daily, how to move on from events and situations that appear to be holding them back, take time out for themselves and alleviate the stresses and strains of everyday life. These are proving to be popular and numbers are increasing each time. I may even have to relocate to larger rooms soon!!

I hold children's relaxation classes – incorporating mindfulness, wellbeing and generally sessions for children to use their imagination and creativity in visualising a beautiful place to go to and therefore encouraging calm. One of my goals is to hold these classes in schools and colleges as I'm a great believer in early intervention.

MY HYPNOTHERAPY PRACTICE

Since graduating, I have started to build my business as a Clinical Hypnotherapist and NLP Practitioner (as well as my other qualifications). This entails attending many networking events, which in truth, I enjoy as I'm a proper chatter box. I love meeting new people and telling them what I do for a living. I'm very passionate about what I do and it shows when I talk. Attending events has given me more confidence to stand and talk about my profession. I no longer dread walking into a room on my own, not knowing a soul. In truth I embrace these times and walk in with power and grace. My life has changed dramatically both professionally and personally. I'm no longer the pessimist. I'm an optimist. I believe in the power of the Law of Attraction and practice it daily. I have a fantastic family who supports me and believes in what I do. They want me to succeed just as much as I do.

I'm still working on improving my practice and will continue to do so, evolving with new evidence, best practices etc., dispelling the myths and misconceptions surrounding Hypnotherapy. My intention is to specialise in Paediatrics. Helping our young children to be children and not carry the burden of the world along with them. Showing them how to leave the past behind, exactly where it belongs and look forward to their futures.

Mostly though, I love being one of Brian's million. I am one in a million.

950799950701

CONTACT DETAILS:

Name:	Les Roberts
Telephone:	(07464) 099447
Email:	lesrobertshypno@sky.com
Website:	
Facebook:	www.facebook.com/lesrobertshypnotherapynlp/

AMANDA HOPPER: AMANDA HOPPER HYPNOTHERAPY

BEFORE BECOMING A HYPNOTHERAPIST

From little acorns!

It isn't often, if ever, that we take a step back, leave the household chores, stop thinking about what to make the family for dinner, and truly reflect on the wondrous journey we have travelled. How did we arrive here, today, suspended in this moment, moulded into the person who is standing in our shoes, often bearing no inward resemblance of the person we once were?

As I sit here, looking back at my journey, I am so full of gratitude, pride and wonder at what I have managed to achieve, things I once would never have conceived as being remotely possible, for no other reason than my belief, in me.

Events have a habit of shaping our lives, both in a good way, and at times in a bad way, often for reasons we are not fully aware of at the time. It is part of our journey, part of our destiny; it is what makes us who we are. We all have our individual stories; our trials and tribulations and life can be a constant test of our resolve. After what can only be described as a shaky start, I have come to know me, love me and believe in me, discovering what I am truly capable of……. and so my story begins.

Having lived with depression for as long as I can remember, even as far back as my childhood, I understand the impact this illness can have on your life. From an early age I suffered from very low self-esteem, with little or no confidence, which resulted in me finding it excruciatingly difficult to form any kind of relationship. Constantly fighting an inward battle, left little or no time for anything else. I never felt I was good enough, I missed a great deal of school, which resulted in me missing out on the gift of education, finally leaving school with no qualifications.

Daily life for me was daunting, filling me with fear and self-doubt. Finding myself in any kind of social situation where I would be expected to interact with other people, either known or unknown to me was particularly difficult. However, against all the odds, age 16, I met and fell in love with my first true boyfriend. This was a momentous point in my life, I truly loved him with all of my heart, but sadly my lack of confidence, my insecurities and my low self-esteem killed our relationship. This is one of my all-time regrets, my lack of belief in me, my lack of love for me, destroyed the one thing and the one person I most wanted and went on to have a few bad relationships.

At the tender age of 18, I was a single parent, living in council flats in Macclesfield. On and off a range of medication in an attempt to treat my depression I sought every kind of counselling out there, but I was on a downward spiral. Now finding myself with a child to support, no qualifications to speak of and armed only with common sense I managed to get some free training and that led to a job with the NHS in IT support. I used each day as a learning opportunity gradually stepping up to the next rung on the ladder. After a hard and arduous journey working my way up over six years or so, I was promoted to the NHS cancer services department. This was a particularly emotional and often stressful role but also incredibly rewarding.

During this time of my life, my path crossed with a lady who was training to be a hypnotherapist, she was asking for volunteers to assist her with the practical aspect of her course. In for a penny, in for a pound, happy to help out, I decided to give it a go and was absolutely amazed. The first thing that astounded me was the fact that I could actually be hypnotised. It was truly fascinating, it intrigued me. I found that after experiencing hypnotherapy, I had a new found confidence. I was empowered, I found myself doing things I wouldn't have ever considered. I was entertaining ideas that would normally be so far removed from what had been my comfort zone, it completely took me by surprise, there was a glimmer of belief, and albeit small there was a glimmer of hope.

Once the voluntary sessions came to an end, sadly at this time, I neither valued myself nor understood hypnotherapy's true potential enough to continue see her.

After working for the NHS for ten years, buying a house and providing a home to raise my beautiful daughter, at the age of 36 and still living in Macclesfield, I hit an all-time low. I found myself back in counselling, back on medication but I was severely fractured and my mind completely broke. I had a total breakdown only able to perform the basic functions needed to exist, this was my darkest moment. The fragile walls of confidence that I had managed to build shattered all around me, I was a prisoner of my past.

I desperately wanted to move through the darkness, which engulfed me. I was in a tragic and awful place, a place I had vowed I would never return to. Recognising my job was a contributing factor to my predicament, I knew I could not remain there, but also knew I could not afford to live where I did without a high paid job. By this time my daughter was thinking of heading off to university, so with no ties and no reason to stay I took a huge leap of faith, sold my house and moved

300 miles away. I knew little about the Berwick upon Tweed; other than I had been there on holiday a few times and felt a calmness and sense of being home when I was there.

To say this was daunting is a resounding understatement. I knew no-one, but I bought a house with much smaller mortgage and with the cost of living so much cheaper, I settled in to my new life. But I carried my depression with me like a large trunk of doom, gloomily pulling it along behind me – I owned it. I had no conception of the damage we can inflict when we find ourselves trapped by our own behaviour and our past problems. I didn't know then that it was my choice to hold on to it. The demons and mistakes of the past need to be left behind, where they belong.

In general, my new life was good, despite some struggles and some low times, there was hope, a shimmer of light in the darkness, showing me how life could be. With a happier, more positive outlook I met a man, only the second man I have ever loved. I was re-energised, and this time I wanted to make an effort, I wanted to battle the insecurities, I desperately wanted to let him into my world. As our relationship developed, I started to feel a modicum of security. I started to think about a career rather than a job, something I really wanted to do, something I felt passionate about, rather than something I had to do.

MY HYPNOTHERAPY TRAINING

Having lived through some tormented years, I wanted to help others; I wanted to provide a place of refuge from the big daunting world we live in. It was my daughter who provided the answer in the shape of an advert she had seen from Innervisions School of Clinical Hypnosis, offering a free weekend to explore hypnotherapy and to experience what it was to be a hypnotherapist. Not only was this a totally FREE event, the weekend was to be held in York, where my daughter was living at the time. The typical old me emerged, sceptical as ever, what was to be gained from a FREE weekend, other than a hard sell, it was after all free so it couldn't be up to much, could it? It wasn't just that, even the thought of having to interact with strangers in an unknown and unfamiliar environment terrified me. Putting all that aside, I booked in anyway; it would be a chance to spend some time with my daughter if nothing else.

As it turned out, and completely unexpectedly, that weekend changed my life, I know how corny that sounds, but it was quite simply the truth. I revelled in the experience of meeting lovely, down to earth, real people. There was no hard sell, but like me there were other sceptics. When the weekend came to a close, I was one of only 3 people who didn't sign up. For me, the only reason being was that I considered it unlikely that I would be able to commit to the training weekends, only getting one weekend off in 3 in my job at the time, and that wasn't a fixed weekend. I just couldn't see how it would be possible for me to pursue this any further. I left feeling so low, a missed opportunity, something so important, but just out of my grasp, it was a very hard and demoralising train journey home.

With memories and thoughts of the weekend still foremost in my mind, I took a chance and mentioned it to my employer, I guessed if I didn't at least ask the question, then I would never be able to honestly say to myself, I had explored every possibility. To my absolute amazement, it was not a problem, my employer said they would support me in any way they could and they would find a way of covering the weekends. This was all the encouragement I needed, a big green light, the go ahead to follow my dream, to do something for me, which would ultimately help other people, and so without any further hesitation I signed up and became an Innervisions student!

I was ecstatic, filled with hope, energised, but also terrified and nervous all at the same time, it felt so right. So, from this point, I feel I must apologise as there will be many clichés, I hate to use them and if I were you reading this I would be tutting and rolling my eyes, but it would be so hard to describe my experience, what happened to me over the year that followed without using them.

HOW MY LIFE CHANGED AFTER BECOMING A HYPNOTHERAPIST

I embarked on my journey and found myself joined on the training course with some truly amazing people, all of us trained and mentored by a fantastic tutor. As the sessions unfolded and after each weekend spent training I started to learn so much about myself, I learnt the complexities of how my mind works and more importantly how I let my mind work against me. As the time unfolded and we journeyed further into the training I started to learn the power of thought and how to use my mind to get what I want from life, to determine whether I had a good day or bad day. I started to understand the importance of letting things go, not holding on to the negatives, I cared less about what people thought, and for the very first time ever, I started to like myself.

I must stress, none of this was easy and it didn't happen overnight, it wasn't instant, it was a journey. With the support of Shirley my course tutor and my fellow students I experienced an amazing year of discovery, learning acceptance, feeling true happiness, but not without shedding some tears, tears that were all part of the learning and healing process. Even if, at the end of the year, had I never practiced hypnotherapy as a business, my time at Innervisions would have still have been worthwhile and not one minute wasted. For the first time ever, I was finally accepting me, accepting who I was and taking control of my thoughts, my feelings and finally banishing my demons. It was a revelation, I discovered whatever your past, your future doesn't have to hold the same, tomorrow can be different, if you choose – it's your choice to make.

I am not going to tell you that I don't get down days, I do, I'm human, I get angry days and emotional days, but what is so different is that I no longer live with depression. I am in charge of me, of my reactions and my choices. This feeling is empowering, I have learnt about the law of attraction, I recognised how it had been working for me all of my life in a negative way, I developed the skills to turn it around and have it work for me in a positive way. I started to think of the good things I wanted out of life, every day I gave thanks for what I had, I opened my mind, my eyes and my heart to opportunity.

My training with Innervisions, together with the life skills I had obtained along the way furnished me with the understanding and the empathy needed to work with a wide range of people, who like me, having lived with depression and low self-esteem had let anxiety and panic rule their lives. Having lost control of their lives they just didn't know how to take back the control. I started my Hypnotherapy practice in a summer house in the garden. I was full of optimism for what the future held. I distributed leaflets locally, set up a business Facebook and a website page.

As the number of clients grew, I found a room to rent above a sports centre, a great offer that only took a small percentage of my income, and I only paid when I used the room. However, it still just wasn't quite right. Living in a rural area, I found a great scheme in a local town offering start-up businesses a workspace at an affordable rate. I could either wait until I had enough clients to cover the monthly rent, or I could act like I already had those clients and take the space – I took the space.

Within a matter of weeks my client base increased, with more and more clients I never had to find the money to pay the rent. My world opened up, I met more people, met fellow therapists and my horizons broadened, I learnt new things, I grew, I thrived.

I was still working part time in administration and part time as a hypnotherapist, I wasn't quite where I needed to be, then from nowhere an opportunity opened up, right in front of my eyes. This was a total life change for my husband and I – yes, I got married, that person who couldn't form a relationship never mind hold onto one, the woman who thought she was worthless, got married!

The opportunity presented itself as a large detached property and two acres of land available for rent, a myriad of opportunities and possibilities all laid out before me. This presented another huge leap into the unknown, a huge financial commitment, a commitment of time and resources, a delicious adventure beckoned. I put together a business plan to run the house as a guest house with thoughts of converting one room into a therapy room. My mind reeled with the possibilities of being able to offer true retreats, a rural getaway, holidays offering the promise of finding yourself, time to reflect on how we think and behave, offering time to de-stress. The money would be tight and if it didn't work, my husband and I stood to lose a lot. Still with this in mind the opportunity was jumping up and down in front of me with big flashing green lights, a sign to go. We now get to wake up each day in a glorious home. I get to meet amazing people and on top of all this I get to live my dream and work as a hypnotherapist nestled in the most stunning surroundings.

What I have come to realise is that people are basically the same; they have the same hopes, the same daily challenges and the same dreams. Everyone wants to improve their life, they want to provide, they want to be happy and ultimately create a better and more hopeful future. Everyone claims to be different, but scratch the surface and surprisingly you will always find similarities.

I see and treat a number of clients. I help people discover themselves and help them to make the simple choice to be happy enabling them to start living the lives they want to live.

Explaining to someone that they have a choice, a very simple choice – be happy or don't, it really is that simple, but had someone said that to me in my darkest times, I would have walked out, I would have thought to myself, you have no idea, you don't know what it's like, you don't know how hard it is - but I do, I have been there, I have made that choice, and no, it wasn't easy, it was hard, it was emotional, it challenged me in every way possible but it is that simple. Through hypnotherapy I exorcised my demons and came out the other side. So I can with the utmost conviction say I understand my clients, I feel their fears, their worries and concerns, and by working together we achieve great things. I don't have a favourite client, a best outcome.

Everyone who I have helped make whatever change they needed to make to turn their lives around is a favourite.

A young girl, excellent swimmer, full of nerves and self-doubt will be swimming the full length of Loch Lomond, a challenge she has set herself and is greatly looking forward to.

A Granny who had a fear of drowning and water since a childhood prank gone wrong, now enjoys taking her grandchildren to the pool, has been kayaking down the Nile and has booked her dream holiday of an arctic cruise to see the Polar bears.

One young lady who tore her eyelashes out to relieve stress flutters her beautiful long lashes at me whenever she sees me.

A friend felt so inspired he too went to Innervisions, and not only became a great hypnotherapist but has joined the team to become a world class tutor.

All of you reading this will interpret my story in your own way, you will feel what you want to feel and think what you want to think, I can only share my story with you. I am not responsible for your thoughts, just my own. That is the biggest lesson I have learnt. As long as I am true to myself, and live my life in a kind, honest, caring way, being thoughtful and considerate of others, I have now learnt to accept that if someone doesn't like me for who I am, then it is their responsibility – not mine!

I hope for those of you reading this chapter of this book, that my words have resonated profoundly. There will of course be the sceptics out there, remember I was once one too. I am sure that there will also be those of you who can relate to my words, those of you who have shared a similar shaky start. I hope there will be those of you who feel inspired and will make that all important choice.

THE RETREAT: BROOMHOUSE FARMHOUSE

If anything I have said, anything I have shared has touched you in any way, struck a chord and you feel you would like to see me or talk to me or any of my colleagues then please do get in touch. Come and stay for a few days, take that time out to reflect, experience the peace, the tranquillity and the wellbeing of rural living, open yourself to all of life has to offer. You can find me online and on Facebook.

Life isn't about what happens to you, it's about how you respond to it that ultimately will make the difference.

CONTACT DETAILS:

Name: Amanda Hopper
Telephone: (07729) 195559
Email: info@amandahopperhypnotherapy.co.uk
Website: www.amandahopperhypnotherapy.co.uk
Facebook: www.facebook.com/amandahopperhypnotherapy

PETER WARKE: PETER WARKE HYPNOTHERAPY, SPAIN

BEFORE BECOMING A HYPNOTHERAPIST

Born in the 1950s in the north east of England, the youngest of six children. My father had a manual job and my mother looked after the home, this was quite typical of the majority of the other families in those days.

Growing up with just the normal schooling it would appear that the best any boy from a working class family could aspire to was to 'Learn a Trade' and of course I followed that excellent advice.

So at the age of 16 I began my working life as an apprentice electrician.

All was well in my world in the late 1970's. I had already reached the limit of what I could aspire to. I had a good job and I owned my own house, just like all of the other working class people from my area. The oil industry was booming so I landed myself an 18 month contract in the Shetland Islands. I felt like I had reached utopia. I was married with a daughter and life was good just as society had dictated it should be.

When I returned to the north east from the Shetlands in 1980, things were different. The happy buoyant mood had changed and for the first time in my life I could not find any work and I had to support my family. Change was needed. I started earning a living from anything I could turn my hand to. I worked part time as a musician and a DJ but still struggled.

To find work I moved to the south of England where work was still plentiful, but unfortunately this put a strain on my marriage working so far away from my home and family and the perfect life came crashing down just like so many others at that time. This was a turning point. I began to question why a working class person was limited to a manual job, why did I have such little control over my life?

This is when I moved to Spain seeking... well, I don't know what I was seeking , all I knew was just like so many others around me I was discontent with my situation.

The late 1980s and I had arrived in Spain and there was plenty of work for a young British guy in the thriving tourist Industry and life was happy and carefree again. I realised that the limits that were set by my peers and parents were not binding and I began to question everything that I had been taught. I was living in a place that reminded me of the movies, blue skies, golden sands, palm trees. There is more and it is there for anyone brave enough to step up and take it.

Lesson #1 Question everything.

Lesson #2 You do not have to be constrained by the limits set by other people.

Lesson #3 Sometimes hardship can bring about positive change.

I had achieved more than the limits set by upbringing, and you know what? You can too!

MY HYPNOTHERAPY TRAINING

I started training as a Clinical Hypnotherapist in 2015, but the real question is why? Why I trained as a Clinical Hypnotherapist? This is a good question.

Lesson #1 taught me to question everything. This came in useful not just for myself but for other people.

Imagine this, friends sitting around the table chatting about their issues in life and of course everyone would have an immediate opinion of what they should do, except for me I would listen to what everyone had to say and wonder why each person offered different advice. I came to the conclusion that each person could only advise based upon their own perspective. The language patterns from everyone spoke louder that their actual words. I would sit and listen quietly before giving my opinion and by doing this quite often this would bring a new perspective to the issue at hand. I lost count of the times when someone would state "you should be a therapist" Yeah, right, me a therapist?

Like so many of us now I use social media and the internet and I began to see advertising for a free weekend to wet ones appetite regarding signing up for a Hypnotherapy course. I'm not stupid I knew that the intention was to entice me to sign up for the full course.

Yeah, right, me a therapist? One of my current jobs at this time was commission only sales and I thought that I could learn something about how they would sell the course. I am always willing to learn something new especially how to sell and after all, it was FREE!

I booked my place on the free weekend. Yeah, right, me a therapist?

Day one Saturday morning and a small group of strangers meet at a lovely Villa in La Nucia. I had only travelled ten minutes to get there, others had journeyed for over an hour. Quite a mixed bunch and we were welcomed into a stranger's home and offered a choice of various beverages, and biscuits.

Brian (Innervisions Principal) introduced himself and began to tell us about himself and how he attained the position he held today. He said that his mission in life is to be instrumental in helping one million people before he dies. He then went on to explain the history of hypnosis, what hypnosis is and how it can be used to enhance the lives of everyone. We were encouraged to ask questions and the atmosphere was relaxed and fun. Brian made the world of hypnosis sound so interesting, exciting and also lucrative.

When I got home that evening I could hardly contain my excitement, I had learned that hypnosis is scientific and not just a bit of mumbo jumbo. I needed to know more. Day two could not come fast enough.

Day two I already felt at home when I entered Brian's Villa on that beautiful Sunday morning. We were given more information but also practical demonstrations of hypnosis. To watch hypnosis being used for practical reasons is astonishing.

I remember thinking that it must take years to learn how to even hypnotise someone. After lunch on that Sunday the whole class learned how to hypnotise someone.

We were separated into pairs and under strict supervision, we all hypnotised each other for the very first time. I had been given; free of charge, the most powerful tool in the world... Now I needed the whole training manual. I needed to be able to use this awesome power with care and compassion. Yes yes yes this was for me, I was hooked.

With hindsight I have to say this was one of my best decisions I have ever made. Module one complete I had my notes and strict instructions to practice, practice, practice and stick to the script. (just try and stop me.) Hurry up! Come on, I want module two and more scripts. In module two when we were informed that we don't need a script I asked the dumbest question ever. "How would I know what to say?" This is when the course gets really interesting. We were encouraged to follow the clients lead and allow ourselves to pick up on tiny clues to guide us what to say.

"(You're My) Soul and Inspiration"

During training, we were taught to listen carefully to our clients. Not to their story, but to their unique language patterns, listening out for subtle clues.

"When"

All of the time

"I wonder why"

Their language patterns often speak louder than their words.

Using this technique you will never ever be…

"In above your head "
"Remember Then"
"You've got what it takes"

Let's play… Using the clues in the phrases above, what can you determine from my language patterns?

Got it yet?

Here is a clue, it's about my other line of work and passion?

Need another clue?

Think song titles from the 70's era…

"step two"

"under the moon of love"

Think album titles...

"I love rock and roll"
"Crepes and drapes"
"Bright lights"
"Good times"

You must have guessed by now they all relate to the legendary 70's band

SHOWADDYWADDY.

Not only do I love rock and roll music, but I sing and dance in a tribute band called 'Shoewaddywaddy' in Benidorm Spain. (Notice the subtle but important extra "E" to change the name of the band.)

Living so close to Benidorm where there are so many cabaret venues it would be rude not to perform.

So, "as a lifetime and passionate entertainer, why doesn't he do a comedy hypnosis show?" (I hear you ask) Well, the answer is simple; I leave the comedy to the best comedienne in Benidorm, my lovely wife, Jenny Renn!

If you are ever visiting Benidorm, come and see the show, and pull me up to say hello!

I will leave this chapter with one more album title. "Next chapter"

MY FAVOURITE CLIENT DURING TRAINING.

We were encouraged to find volunteers to allow us to practice our newly learned skills from each module. I had plenty of people interested in smoking cessation and slimming and I did say that they could have this done for free once I get to that part of the course, if they would allow me to practice on them every week.

One person who volunteered had arthritis and was quite clearly in pain and I had observed a pain relief method in class so thought can't do the smoking thing yet so why not address the pain issue.

This was quite successful and we had been told that the subconscious mind controls the physical body and decided to do some research on osteoarthritis I found details of an operation called an Arthroscopy. I downloaded the information to use on the next session. Under hypnosis I described the operation being done on the arthritic joint and after the session there was an immediate improvement. The following week we did the same procedure again and this time the symptoms were completely gone. Just two sessions and all the pain and symptoms of the arthritis gone.

We were running out of issues to address so we turned to what do you want to have in your life that you don't have now. The answer was a loving permanent relationship. Why not? what is there to lose?

During this session I started with a basic plan and then just went away from the original intention, I don't know why, but we were taught follow your instincts so I did. I just seemed to know what to say as I started making up a story, filled with metaphors and then there was a choice to make one choice would lead to a new life with the loving partner and the other choice would be to continue on the same life.

The choice was between two doors. Just before I said choose the one you want, I put a no smoking sign on the door to the new happy life.

It would appear that this person wanted a happy loving relationship so badly that they gave up the cigarettes instantly. I am typing this with tears running down my cheeks as I re-live that moment, we know what to say because we can feel the emotions of the client. This person is now in that loving relationship and has never smoked since. Sometimes the emotions can be overwhelming, not always but you need to be ready for anything. Notes to self,

1. Always have a box of tissues in the therapy room

2. Find an office to work from so things are more private

Only part the way through the course and I find out how important it is to be professional and needed to rent a consulting room. Time now for the Law of Attraction to work its magic!

Shortly after this I had a message to go and see someone regarding renting a room for occasional use, however it turns out that there was a bit of a communication breakdown, this person wanted hypnotherapy and had heard that I was in training, could I help?

I went down to talk about renting a room and they said yes they did have a room but that was not the reason they called. Wow talk about two birds with one stone. The issue they wanted me to work on had already been covered on the course and they had used hypnosis for other issues and had every confidence that it would work.

So I now have a great place to work from and started to do group hypnosis sessions (guided meditation) and got paid for doing them. I was assured at the start of the course that it is possible to earn back the cost of the course even before you complete it. I did this with ease, it is easier to charge for your services when you are working from a posh business premises.

On the day I graduated and had my third certificate to put up on my wall. Module one certificate, Hypnoslimmer certificate and now my graduation certificate. The most important thing about my graduation is the knowledge that there is backup and help if I feel that I need anything. Brian is always ready to offer any help in any way.

MY HYPNOTHERAPY PRACTICE

Since graduation and have attended many other additional courses to build on the firm foundation of my initial course. You can never have too many tools at your disposal. I moved from my initial premises to somewhere closer to home where I had my own keys allowing me to be able to see clients outside of normal business hours. My clients want confidentiality and privacy, along with a professional but friendly service. The place I was in previously was good but not perfect. With this in mind I started my search for a better location. I use the law of attraction for everything (thank you Brian yet another wonderful thing that you taught me) The new location in Callosa D'en Sarria just seemed to appear from nowhere I went to look at it and was so excited that I went straight over to Brian's house to tell him all about it. A small clinic with a private entrance. Everything self-contained, private office leading to a very comfortable air-conditioned consultation room. Small enough to be cosy but big enough to hold small groups. Clients with sensitive issues can enter without anyone asking awkward or potentially embarrassing questions. Brian was not at home when I called round, but one of his top tutors, Donna Jenkinson was there waiting for delivery of some new office equipment.

Donna was also looking for a new consulting room; this was perfect as this new place is big enough for both of us. How lucky am I not only the perfect premises but having one of the top clinical hypnotherapists in Spain working alongside me. The future is truly looking bright. All this from answering a small advert for a free weekend course!

The lessons leaned on the course and the subsequent additional courses have changed my life. I have learned that you can have everything you want to make you happy. I have learned that there is abundance of everything for everybody. I have learned that you, yes **YOU!** have the right to be happy. I have learned that I can now use the knowledge and skills that I now possess to earn a living by enhancing the lives of others.

I feel extremely honoured to be part of Brian's dream of helping one million people during his lifetime.

Thank you Brian.

CONTACT DETAILS:

Name: Peter Warke
Telephone: (+34) 602 21 55 18
Email: peterwarke@hotmail.com
Facebook: www.facebook.com/peter.warke.hypnosis

HILARY MOULDS: HILLARY MOULDS CLINICAL HYPNOTHERAPY

BEFORE BECOMING A HYPNOTHERAPIST

If you had suggested 10 years ago, I would become a hypnotist, I would have laughed and probably not very nicely!

I was working as an HR Director in the big banks in London – tough contracts, mega bucks. I had a great social life and loved London. I'd moved to London when I was 24, from Hull. A very (at the time) deprived city, not a coffee shop in sight back in the 80s and yes, I'm 54!

Then one day, I fought my way home on the tube, opened a bottle of wine and thought 'where the heck did everyone go?' My friends had got married and moved further out as they had children, I was contracting, so I didn't get invited to the works parties or do's. I realised, I was actually a bit lonely.

The next weekend, I went home to see my parents and when I really looked at them, I was shocked to see how old they looked.

Back in the city on the Monday morning, 2012, I stood up all the way to work on the tube, some random guy pressed firmly against my bottom (who says London isn't friendly) and by the time I got to the office, I wasn't in a great mood. Now, if you've ever worked in HR you will know that you get to deal with some challenging individuals. That morning I was having a discussion with one of those individuals who. I was pretty sure because of his volatility that he was on coke anyway, and then I just felt something break. I knew, there and then, London was finished. I'd had enough of being shouted at because someone else had stuffed up. Done finished!

Whilst I finished my contract (hey I'm professional), I looked for a place to rent not far from mum and dad in Hull and put my house on the market.

Fast forward to 2013, now in Yorkshire; the job situation in East Yorkshire in 2013 was not good. Understatement perhaps! I went from being hugely marketable to virtually unemployable in my field of expertise. I took a contract in Birmingham for 12 months and travelled for hours every week but that was ok, I was used to it. I was still lonely though. I took classes at night, and studied counselling. Finished my contract in Birmingham, took other smaller, HR jobs, and hated them.

MY HYPNOTHERAPY TRAINING

In 2015, knowing another contract was ending, I was looking for alternative employment, and I saw an advert for a free hypnotherapy training weekend with Innervisions School of Clinical Hypnosis. Yeah, Yeah, Free? Hypnosis? Ha Ha..... mmmm ok, its free, I have nothing to lose, if I hate it, I won't go back on the Sunday. I've been hooked ever since!

We learned to hypnotise each other! It was FAB. I was so amazed and impressed that I decided to take the whole practitioner level training course. One weekend a month over the following 10 months.

I qualified in October 2015, but I'd been practicing my new found hypnotic skills on volunteers from week one on the advice of out tutor. Then I started seeing clients, whilst still working part time in HR

During this time I was working at the Humber Bridge and I loved working there. My boss who was the Bridgemaster was lovely. The Board were very kind to me when I became ill. My colon ruptured and I needed emergency surgery. Clients cancelled, feet up in hospital, March to June 2016, at home recovering from a colostomy op.

Amazingly, my lovely boss asked me to go back. During October 2016 I was back in hospital. My tiny stream of clients once again put on hold as I had another operation to start the reversal process of having a colostomy. Off work again till December 2016. When I got back to work I was told that my boss was leaving we and that we had a new Chief Exec starting soon. Sad, but change happens. Then fast forward to May 2017 I had a very good contract at the Humber Bridge even though half the time I wasn't getting paid as I was recovering from ops. But I had a really good run, did I tell you I LOVE that bridge ha ha. I was given a date for the final stage of my reversal, my Chief Exec kindly told me to go and I could come back which I did, but only for a week. The Board unfortunately, said no more contractors. That was it, I finished at the Bridge 30 June 2017.

As I put my feet up the week after, I decided, no way was anyone ever having control over my income ever again but me. This was it, I was setting up full time as a hypnotherapist.

HOW MY LIFE CHANGED AFTER BECOMING A HYPNOTHERAPIST

10 July 2017 (ok I had 2 weeks off ish) I opened as a full time Hypnotherapy Practitioner. Terrifying, how would I get clients, pay bills or feed the cats? I might hate it! I can't lie, it WAS stressful. I had no savings, no income at times other than the odd client coming in. But I gritted my teeth, I'd been through worse (remember the property crash in 2008/9, yep, I was there!). I sold lots of stuff on Ebay, I didn't go out much, and I did wonder what the hell I was doing occasionally. Until a client came in and I thought, god I love doing this! Well (dear readers) I LOVE IT, best decision EVER. In just four months, I have enough clients to fill two full days, so I'm looking forward to 2018 three days will sort me. I still have my mum to think about. I don't miss my corporate life, I will never say I will never do corporate again as I might, as a hypnotist, but I love being in control of my own life and my own income.

What do I do with the rest of my time? Whatever I want! See mum, see friends yes, I have friends! And I see them. I'm not miles away and lonely like I was before. Now I'm happy and busy. I get the chance to do stuff I've never done, like contribute to books! and who knows, maybe I'll write my own one day!

I don't get Mondayitis anymore. I love opening my diary and seeing who is coming in to see me that day. I meet some fab people and get to help people from all walks of life. Some things thrill me because they mean so much to the person you are helping.

CLIENT SUCCESS STORY ONE

I remember the bride to be who had bitten her nails from being a child, all she wanted was beautiful nails on her big day. She got them, because of me. She got them because she got the courage up to come to a hypnotherapist.

CLIENT SUCCESS STORY TWO

I help lots of clients who want to reduce their shape and size. I had one client who sticks in my mind. She had been overweight all her life. She went through my four week Hypnoslimmer Weight Control programme which I learned in training. She came out the other side and carried on and she's now three sizes smaller. Her life has changed because of the program, she's a great ambassador for me, more importantly, she is the size she wants to be now. And THAT'S the important thing!

I view every successful treatment as a win. I meet some fabulous people and I'm really really happy that I can help them.

MY HYPNOTHERAPY PRACTICE

I now have a beautiful private clinic here in Cottingham, Hull. It's bright, comfortable and airy. I offer all hypnotherapy treatments and have an excellent success record with the amazing Hypnoslimmer weight control system. I also specialise pain management. I am also a qualified counsellor and offer other treatments including Reiki.

I am proud to have trained with Innervisions School of Clinical Hypnosis, who are one of the UK's top training providers and I am humbled to play an active role in Brian Glenn's lifetime quest to help one million people. One of my many strengths is my professional, patient and down to earth approach whilst at the same time maintaining a very compassionate and non-judgemental focus. I am really passionate about people connecting with who they truly are and getting the best out of life and take great pride in my success and ability to really connect with everyone whom I work with.

Whatever the problem, feel free to contact me if you would like to take advantage of a completely free and unconditional consultation.

CONTACT DETAILS:

Name: Hilary Moulds
Telephone: (07721) 652440
Email: enquiries@hilarymoulds.com
Website: www.hilarymoulds.com
Facebook: www.facebook.com/hilary.moulds

TEE LIBURD: TOGETHERNESS THERAPY

When I was asked to contribute to my hypnotherapy tutors' book I was immensely honoured. I'm aware that my tutor, Brian Glenn's, dream was to touch a million people through Hypnosis. In over 21 years as a therapist, trainer, author of a number of books and owner of Innervisions School of Clinical Hypnosis my admiration for this man meant that I could not say no to this opportunity.

In my professional life I know that I have personally touched the lives of thousands of people and know how rewarding it can be to see the changes my impact has had on those people I have been in contact with. Whether it be by providing music as a DJ, or providing support services to disadvantaged people, or providing training to staff employed in public services, or through my Hypnotherapy and complementary therapies the self-satisfaction has been immense.

In 2008 I was told by a medium I went to see that I would write at least two books in my lifetime. Although I've thought about doing this I've never managed to start writing. This opportunity has given me the perfect springboard to looking at taking book writing more seriously as I've found this experience to be very cathartic. I feel I am now ready to share my life experiences with others in the hope that I can support them in making positive changes to their lives.

BEFORE BECOMING A HYPNOTHERAPIST

I am the ninth born child of my Mother and Father and my entry into this world was unconventional. My Mother, who had already had eight children, was waiting for my arrival whilst sat on a bed in the Maternity ward. My Mother could sense that I was due to arrive and called one of the nurses to let her know that I was due to arrive. The nurse didn't believe my Mother and advised that my Mother wait in the ward as she wasn't ready to deliver me. A few moments later my Mother called the nurse again, this time the nurse took notice of her, placed her into a wheelchair and proceeded to wheel my Mother into the delivery suite.

Whilst wheeling my Mother to the delivery suite the nurse got called away and left my Mother in the corridor. My Mother told me that she felt so ashamed as I was delivered in the corridor in full view of a couple of contractors who were decorating the corridor. This is how I came into this world. Whilst most babies were able to bond with their Mothers after being delivered I wasn't afforded that opportunity as I was whisked away as the delivery caused me to land on the concrete floor, causing blood to spurt from my damaged mouth. I believe that we all experience some trauma in our lives and for me this traumatic experience had a very profound effect on my life.

In 2015 I was given the opportunity to go to the USA to train with some of the world's top entrepreneurs in the field of Referral Marketing. Whilst attending the training I shared the experience of my birth with business owners across the world, explaining in detail what had happened and the impact it had on me. I shared with my fellow business owners the reason why I do what I do as a profession. Not being able to bond with my Mother gave me a feeling of loneliness, not being loved and accepted, and this caused me to having feelings of abandonment throughout my life. This resulted in me not being able to maintain long relationships and allowed me to recognise that there must be other people in this world who had similar experiences. This is 'My Why', and the main reason why I do what I do. I love supporting those who have feelings of abandonment, not being able to love and accept themselves, not knowing how to make positive changes in their lives in the same way as I have.

When I was about eight years old I remember sitting in the living room one day and had this overwhelming feeling that I was Jesus Christ. I had a very religious upbringing, attending Sunday school at the Methodist churches I attended from a very early age. At the same time I noticed white lights from the corner of my eyes circulating the room, which I found strange, but not phased by this experience. This experience made me question whether there was something wrong with me, and I didn't feel able to share this experience with my parents nor with any of my siblings. Reflecting on this experience and having researched these types of phenomena made me realise that I was having some kind of spiritual awakening.

I spent my school years supporting friends who were being bullied at school, in particular friends who had just arrived in the UK having being expelled from Uganda by the Idi Amin regime. For the majority of my professional life my employment has involved supporting, advising and guiding members of the public whether it be providing financial, physical and emotional support.

Whilst residing in Leicester I was employed by the Civil Service providing financial assistance to applicants who were unemployed or on low incomes. At that time I was heavily involved in politics, supporting miners whilst they were on strike and being financially destitute. This was the first time that I experienced racial discrimination, having been the first person of African descent to be employed by the organisation.

I spent 27 years working as a public servant working for a number of local authorities and housing associations. I thoroughly enjoyed this profession as it continued to allow me to support members of the public who faced homelessness, those who resided in accommodation which wasn't suited to their needs, experienced financial difficulties or faced discrimination due to their housing situation. I also supported those that faced racial discrimination daily. I was fortunate enough to be employed as Equality and Diversity Manager, where I was able to influence the organisations' policies and procedures to ensure that service users did not face discrimination based on their age, disability, gender, race, religion, sexual orientation. I enjoyed the challenge as I was able to train staff employed by the organisation, making them aware of their rights and responsibilities to ensure that service users were treated according to their needs without being discriminated against.

MY HYPNOTHERAPY TRAINING

Training to become a Professional Clinical Hypnotherapist happened by a synchronistic meeting with a friend who I had previously attended a Counselling Skills training course with. I met my friend whilst on a bus and she seemed really excited as she had just completed the training with the Innervisions School of Clinical Hypnosis and suggested that I apply to go on the course. The reason being because during our Counselling Skills training she said that I came across as a caring, considerate and compassionate human being and that I would be great at supporting those who had physiological and emotional issues.

I applied to attend the free weekend thinking that the course was going to be oversubscribed and that my application wouldn't be successful. Imagine my excitement when I received confirmation that I was invited along to the free weekend. I was very sceptical about Hypnotherapy as my only experience was being hypnotised by the world renowned hypnotist, Paul McKenna.

When I took part in his stage hypnotist session, which was carried out live on MTV in front of 250,00 viewers across Europe. I found the whole experience to be very strange and I didn't feel I was being put under hypnosis; however, what I understand about hypnosis now makes me believe that I was. I found the whole experience to be safe, non-obtrusive and I was a willing participant as I saw myself as a bit of an exhibitionist.

The training provided by the Innervisions School of Clinical Hypnosis was very informative and the information provided I found very easy to understand. What I loved most about the training was it gave me the opportunity to practice and apply the skills obtained not only to myself but to those who wanted to change the way that they felt about their emotional and physiological wellbeing.

I decided to train because I am passionate about helping those who want to live a more fulfilled and happier life. I already hold qualifications in providing complementary therapies to others, i.e. Reiki Practitioner to Masters Level, Swedish Massage Practitioner, Diploma in Counselling Skills and as Volunteer Listener for The Samaritans. I am also a trained Coach providing support services for business owners to allow them to increase their client base, and saw this training as a natural progression to obtaining additional skills and tools to be able to provide more effective support to others.

HOW MY LIFE CHANGED AFTER BECOMING A HYPNOTHERAPIST

Being a Professional Clinical Hypnotherapist has allowed me to look at the things which have held me back in my personal and professional life. I haven't always been the most confident person, having experienced a number of issues in my life, which have prevented me from being the best that I can be. Issues around self-confidence, certain fears and phobias and my ability to sustain long lasting, personal relationships. The skills I now have allow me to support others on a daily basis, whether it be paying clients, or family and friends.

CLIENT SUCCESS STORY

Client X came to see me as she had been experiencing issues with depression, anxiety, self-harming, low confidence and self-esteem. Client X was a lone parent with three children. She explained that her upbringing had been very challenging as her father was an alcoholic and her relationship with her siblings wasn't conventional. Client X was also experiencing relationship issues with her existing partner. I recognised that her patterns of behaviour were being repeated.

During the Consultation I was able to recognise how I could deal with my client and provide the most effective way to help her address her issues more effectively. As Client X was taking anti-depressants I sought advise from my Supervisor as to whether I could provide therapy to my client as there may be certain contraindications. Initially, I used techniques to allow her to release the emotional baggage that seemed to be preventing her from being the best that she could be. Subsequent sessions involved lots of imagery and breathing techniques to reduce her anxiety. Within a couple of weeks Client X stated that she had reduced her medication and that her GP appeared impressed by her emotional and physiological wellbeing.

A few weeks into the sessions, Client X advised me that she was due to take part in a national weight lifting competition to qualify for international and world championships, and that she was feeling very anxious about whether she would qualify. In the lead up to the championship I provided more confidence and motivation sessions, and was overwhelmed when Client X notified me that she had qualified to represent her country in 2018 for the European and World Championships to be held in Budapest and Barcelona.

CLIENT SUCCESS STORY TWO

A short time ago, the parents of an eleven old came to see me as their son was exhibiting signs of extreme anxiety. I remember the day they came to see me, and on greeting them in the reception area of my clinic I noticed the young man was rocking backwards and forwards and banging his head consistently with his fists. Their son had recently experienced three traumatic events; he had soiled himself in the school playground, he was being bullied, and his pet cat had died. It was only the second time that I had provided therapy to a young person and my first thoughts were that he was going to be very challenging. I also sensed that he may have been on the autistic spectrum. The parents were waiting for their son to be allocated a Support Worker from the local CAHMS team. He had been excluded from school and was being educated at home by his Mother, which was causing additional strain on the family's' relationship. I saw this client on at least seven occasions, and during the sessions I allowed him to talk about his feelings, and did not provide much hypnotherapy, which seemed to help him considerably. When it was time for him to stop seeing him, his parents could not thank me enough.

As a Professional Clinical Hypnotherapist I find the most rewarding thing is seeing the positive changes my clients have made to their emotional and physiological wellbeing. I have seen hundreds of clients in the short space of time that I have been practising. It has not always been easy obtaining clients, but having acquired certain skills, especially in terms of confidence building, has given me the confidence to attend regular Networking meetings and media interviews, to share with others what I do and how I can help them to take control of their Lives. One of the other rewarding aspects of being a Professional Clinical Hypnotherapist has been able to recommend a number of my clients to become Clinical Hypnotherapists and study with the Innervisions School of Clinical Hypnosis.

MY HYPNOTHERAPY PRACTICE

I set up my practice in 2013 on a part time basis and decided to go full time in 2016. During which time I have seen and helped hundreds of people. I offer therapies to help people manage their issues with anxiety, their relationship with food, smoking cessation amongst other things. I now specialise in anxiety as I see this as a root cause for the issues that my clients might be experiencing. I love attending

Supervision sessions and the wide range of Hypnotherapy training provided by more established Hypnotherapists.

I have recently qualified as a Mental Health First Aider, where I am able to recognise clients who have mental health issues, such as depression, PTSD, anxiety and addictions. This has given me the ability to sign post such clients to other agencies who are more qualified to deal with their issues.

I utilise my interest and understanding of Buddhist principles into my hypnotherapy sessions and find this blend to be most effective.

Also, because I have been practising for a number of years and undertaken CPD I have recently been awarded Senior Practitioner status by one of my governing bodies, the General Hypnotherapy Register.

I continue to provide support as much as possible to those who are serious about improving their emotional and physiological wellbeing. I currently work from my home in Mirfield, West Yorkshire, a very peaceful and scenic setting, and see clients every day of the week.

CONTACT DETAILS

Name: Tee Liburd
Telephone: (07828) 231129
Email: hello@togethernesstherapy.co.uk
Website: www.togethernesstherapy.co.uk
Facebook: www.facebook.com/tee.liburd

LAURA SHEWFELT: YOUR WEIGHT LOSS FAIRY

First, I would like to say that I am incredibly proud to be one of Brian's million, and part of the ripple which will continue infinitely. I look forward to doing my best to help to indirectly contribute to Brian's target for many years to come.

BEFORE BECOMING A HYPNOTHERAPIST

I always wonder in amazement at people who hear their true career calling as a teenager and follow it through for life. For me, it took almost 40 years to realise what my career destiny was. My teenage years and early twenties were spent training in the performing arts and obtaining a degree in Drama and Theatre and treading the boards for a while. But whilst I was passionate about this for a number of years, the universe had other plans for me and I soon found myself married aged 22 and ensconced behind a desk at Barnet Council. Whilst this might sound rather a come down from the dizzy excitement of stage and screen, at this point in my life, I actually really relished the opportunity of making good money, buying a home and laying the foundations for our future family life. My husband was a jobbing actor at this time and I loved the fact that I could provide us with financial stability.

Fast forward a number of years and three kids later, a stint of living in LA as a mortgage consultant where I managed Henry Winkler 'The Fonz' mortgage amongst other things. I then found myself back in London working again in Local Government. This time, however, I was feeling a distinct sense of lack and discontent; I was feeling that my true purpose had yet to be found and that it needed to be quickly! I was, at this time, an avid reader of anything to do with the Law of Attraction and the likes of the book 'The Secret' had become my constant companion. I realised the extreme power of the mind, its potential to make better, its ability to heal the body and itself, its pliability and ability to change. My attention kept being drawn to hypnotherapy in lots of different ways. Related posts on Facebook began to show up in my newsfeed and articles about it would just appear under my nose. I also had recurring dreams where I was 'using my voice'. Dreams where I was actually speaking for long periods of time and knowing within my dream that the words I was saying were incredibly powerful and important. I get that this might sound a bit woo-woo, but I am a firm believer of following the 'signs', listening to my inner wisdom, my intuition and I now know that those dreams were directing me to my purpose, my present career.

MY HYPNOTHERAPY TRAINING

One of the 'signs' that I followed, was to attend a free weekend run by one of the UK's leading hypnotherapy training providers. This was quite honestly one of the best decisions that I have EVER made. I must admit that I was initially sceptical. No one else I could see ran a free two day introduction to hypnotherapy, but that is exactly what it was!

The beauty of attending that two full day introduction was that it reaffirmed to me that I was making the right decision in pursuing the career path and it also gave me an insight into the ethos of that particular training provider. It all resonated massively with me and despite the fact I could have trained far closer to home, I signed up for the Innervisions School of Clinical Hypnosis Nottingham 2013 intake, a decision I will be forever grateful that I made.

HOW MY LIFE CHANGED AFTER BECOMING A HYPNOTHERAPIST

The following ten months were eye opening, intriguing and fundamentally changed many of the ways in which I looked at life. Each month I couldn't wait for the next training weekend to come around. It gave me an extremely comprehensive grounding in psychotherapy and all aspects of clinical hypnotherapy and a great range of tools and techniques on which to draw upon. I also met some great people and some lifelong friends on the course and had tons of fun along the way. For me, it was also important that the course was one recognised by a regulatory body and provided me with a qualification that was actually respected and worth something.

I was surprised and thrilled to find that I began to treat paying clients before the end of the course and I pretty much recouped my course fees by the time I graduated. The success that I had with these early clients really fuelled my belief in my skills and also my desire to become a highly successful full time hypnotherapist.

For the next ten months or so, I juggled my 'day' job and my hypnotherapy practice and took on a room at a local clinic. During this time I saw clients for a variety of issues but predominantly I found that I was attracting a lot of clients for weight loss and it was clear that this was where my greatest talent and interest lay. As time went on my 'day' job became a hindrance to the work that I really wanted to do and so I took the plunge and handed in my notice and focussed on making hypnotherapy my full time occupation.

So, pretty amazingly, in less than a year, I had retrained in a completely new and fulfilling discipline, given up my long term public sector job and set up my own business. Moreover, a business that I could fit around the needs of my three children and family life perfectly.

I decided that niching in a particular area was going to be the best way forward in firmly establishing myself and drawing to me my ideal clients on a consistent basis. I wanted to be the 'go to' person for a specific issue and to that end I began to undertake more training in the area of weight loss. I was already experiencing a good level of client success in this area but I wanted to strengthen my results and ensure that they were sustainable in the long term for the client. To this end, I began working with coach and mentor Steve Miller who is well known in the weight loss industry and hypnotherapy and also host of the CH4 TV series 'Fat Families'. This experience brought me many new tools for my toolbox and also gave me a greater understanding of how to implement effective PR and marketing. As a culmination of this, in August 2014, my brand "Your Weight Loss Fairy" was launched and does exactly what it says on the tin.

CLIENT SUCCESS STORY ONE

Claire was a 42 year old Company Director from Hampshire whose weight on beginning work with me was almost 31 stone. She had been obese for as long as she could remember and recalled being taken along to slimming clubs as a young girl. She believed that she was destined to be fat for life as she had been told this from a young age by her mother (who was also overweight) and who informed her that was simply in her genes. Claire worked long hours in a demanding job and dealt with the stress by eating fast food and chocolate daily and to great excess.

Claire was married with two young children and after a horrendous theme park holiday where she found herself being pushed around by her husband in a wheelchair as she could not handle the walking, found herself in my consulting room, desperate for help and change. Claire had tried to follow diets on numerous occasions and had attended a multitude of slimming clubs but found that it just didn't work for her.

Claire was also suffering frequent panic attacks due to the fact that she realised her weight was highly detrimental to her health and had a constant fear of heart failure.

I agreed to take Claire onto my bespoke six week weight loss programme which was very much tailored to her individual situation. We first of all addressed her anxiety and I taught techniques that she could use if she felt a panic attack arising, we also looked at her core beliefs, attitudes and values that were driving her destructive eating behaviours. Once these had been brought to the surface and dealt with, we began the task of reprogramming her mind set and approach to food and building new, healthy habits and attitudes.

Building Claire's confidence and self-esteem and her belief that she could become a healthy weight was a priority, and developing specific goals and plans to achieve those goals were also key.

At the end of the six week programme, Claire had lost 30lb and had not indulged in fast food or chocolate since session one. Moreover, she did not want to. Claire has since gone on to lose another stone and receives ongoing support from me via text and a face to face session every 4 weeks to ensure that her motivation remains elevated and so that her new, healthy habits are regularly reinforced.

Claire feels like her life has now been unlimited and believes that it is possible for her to become a healthy weight"

I now work with clients both in person and via video call, this means that clients' location is no barrier to my service and my results are proving consistent via both methods. In addition to my own six week tailored programme, I am also a licensed FATnosis Practitioner and am thrilled to have just won the FATnosis Practitioner of 2017 award. The FATnosis Programme is very straight talking, no nonsense approach to weight loss and focuses on three key areas, namely: Mind Programming, Motivational Interventions and the 80/20 Meal Planning System. Clients are assessed for suitability for this programme at consultation.

I am also a certified FATnosis Academy Leader and my recent five week academy achieved a phenomenal cumulative weight loss of 65lb.The Academy is a small weight management group environment where members are provided with tools to kick start and keep will power consistent, learn how to programme their own minds in a strong and motivational way and receive coaching in creative portion control and in the 80/20 lifestyle approach to eating.

CLIENT SUCCESS STORY TWO

Lynda was a 55 year old full time school administrator who arrived at week one of my FATnosis Academy desperate to change habits that were causing her to gain weight on a weekly basis and for her Type 2 Diabetes to worsen. Lynda had a happy and content family life and knew that her problems were purely being caused by her habit of putting too much food into her body. She was absolutely ready to acknowledge and take full accountability for her actions and so was a perfect candidate for a place in the Academy.

Lynda embraced the Academy process wholeheartedly and carried out the homework and technique practice that is required. At the end of the five weeks, she had lost 13lbs and was well on her way to her goal weight. In addition, she had also massively improved her diabetic control. Her hba1c score had dramatically reduced and her doctor had confirmed that with continued weight loss and strengthening of her new lifestyle habits she had the potential to get off prescribed medication and reverse the diagnosis"

In early 2017, after again following the signs, I decided that the time was right to establish my second niche and so I launched the Law of Attraction Coaching Academy. It was, after all, my passion for this subject that had brought me to hypnotherapy in the first place.

A massive thank-you to Brian Glenn, the author of this book, who has played a huge part in all this coming to be. His knowledge and teaching of The Law of Attraction and taking his CPD course 'The Science of Living Your Dreams' has been invaluable to me.

To date, I have run Foundation Masterclasses in Birmingham, London and Manchester with further ones being planned for other areas of the UK very soon. I have discovered that I very much thrive working in a group environment and facilitating and presenting and very much see it as my future path. I am thrilled to have been asked to be a guest speaker on the Law of Attraction at an upcoming weight loss conference and it's exciting to see the cross over between my two passions developing.

I am indeed now 'using my voice' and feel extremely blessed to have had the opportunities and amazing mentors that I have had in my life.

MY HYPNOTHERAPY PRACTICE

My hypnotherapy practice is based in St Albans, Hertfordshire, where I am fortunate to have a tranquil, idyllic parkland as my office backdrop. Clients find the surroundings highly conducive to healing and wellbeing and I myself benefit greatly from the calm and natural setting. In addition to seeing clients who want to lose weight, I also take on a limited number of other clients per month with differing issues. Recently this has included a number of children with anxiety related problems and sleep issues. Helping them to rectify this is profoundly rewarding.

My other special interests lie in helping those with a lack of confidence and self-esteem as these can affect every thought, every feeling and every action a person takes. I find hypnotherapy to be highly effective in making permanent change in these areas. Clients usually progress very quickly and are able to free themselves from worry and inhibitions in so many areas of life, such work, relationships, social situations etc. Breaking down those sub-conscious barriers that are holding people back and stopping them reaching their full potential is really an amazing job to have!

CONTACT DETAILS

Name: Laura Shewfelt
Telephone: (07931) 799025
Email: hello@yourweightlossfairy.com
Website: www.yourweightlossfairy.com
Facebook: www.facebook.com/laura.shewfelt

COLLEEN REA: ANCIENT OAK HYPNOTHERAPY

BEFORE BECOMING A HYPNOTHERAPIST

From a young age I always had the desire to help people. From a child it was playing nurse to soft toys, dolls and much to their dismay my siblings. Life goes on and I left school and found myself working in offices for a couple of years forgetting my dream as a child to be a nurse. It is interesting the path one's life takes; some would say it was fate. I found myself living in a small village with three young children and needing to learn to drive as transport facilities were limited to riding tractors. I got myself a job working in the local nursing home and I this reawakened my desire to be a nurse.

Travelling forward in time a little I wanted to get some experience so working in different areas, so health care assistant in the local hospital was my next stop. I found that my favourite part of my job was spending time talking to people. This would get me into bother with the nurse in charge at times as I was taking too long to make the beds or do the tea round. For me I felt that talking to people and sharing a joke or just 'checking in' with people and exchange pleasantries was as important as any physical intervention but there was no time for this it seemed. I therefore decided that general nursing was not for me and having close relatives with mental health problems I decided that I would go down the route of becoming a registered mental health nurse. I guess there was also a desire to understand myself more in the process and this is something I am still working on to this day.

Twelve years later I am still working in the same profession. So, I have worked in pretty much most areas of mental health, in acute wards, crisis teams and community teams. I currently work in GP surgeries assessing, signposting and advising people. What has become apparent to me over the years and working within the different sectors are the complexities of being human and what that means. I can see 20 people a week with depression but each one of them will present with differing symptoms and the impact on their lives (and that of those closest to them) will also be different.

I have always believed we all have the ability to partially heal ourselves from some ailments and mental health problems. I have seen countless people resign themselves to years of taking pharmacological interventions (medication) as a crutch, scared to even contemplate reducing and stopping the medications in-case they relapse. Don't get me wrong here, there is certainly a place for medication in all areas of medicine whether it is physical health or mental health but there is also a place for psychological approaches too.

I consider myself to be in the very privileged position to be able to listen to people's life stories as part of my job and sometimes they can be truly horrific stories to be told. They can hold on to so much stuff from their past which is still preventing them from moving on in their life and feeling fulfilled as a person. But more than this can be so damaging to them affecting their health in every way. I guess we all hold on to 'baggage' from our past that affects how we live our lives now but what if we could find a way of letting go of some of that 'baggage' and finding a way of moving forward in our lives?

What if we could find a way of being the person that we have always wanted to be? Healthier, successful (which is individual), full of confidence and self-esteem and feel like we have found our place in the world.

I was always looking for therapy tools that I could use to help people achieve the above but had no idea that the next tool I would be choosing would have so much of a positive impact on my own life. The next chapter of life my life was to begin.

MY HYPNOTHERAPY TRAINING

On my Facebook feed (fate again maybe) I saw an advert for Innervisions School of Clinical Hypnosis offering a free weekend in Peterborough. I will admit I was a little sceptical to begin with, having never had hypnotherapy and not really knowing much about it but I was intrigued enough to sign up for this initial weekend.

I was understandably nervous prior to attending this weekend but almost immediately from starting the course I knew I had made the right decision. It is hard work and let's face it anything worth learning is ordinarily hard work, but it is life changing. You do have homework to do but this is to recap on what you may have learned the previous weekend.

The handouts are great and will provide you with the information you need moving forward when practising as a clinical hypnotherapist. Elaine Draper was our tutor in Peterborough and she was both warm, supportive and very professional. There may well be tears along the way, some of joy and some of sorrow (I experienced both) but any journey has its ups and downs, right?

I believe the face to face tuition was invaluable and you had plenty of opportunity to practise your hypnotherapy skills with your tutor guiding you along the way which is something you wouldn't get from online tuition.

When first trying out my hypnotherapy skills I again was nervous and felt very self-conscious and constantly questioning myself such as; was I speaking clearly or loudly enough? and even wondering if I sounded like a complete muppet but Elaine (tutor) put me at ease and by the end of the course I did not even think about it.

So, the course is split into 10 modules which is basically one weekend a month learning a module. For me the time in between modules was good as it gave me the time to practise my learning but also reflect (I am a great reflector) on what we had learned and do further reading on the subject. My family and friends loved the training as they were my guinea pigs. I helped them with various ailments and confidence boosters along the way and this continues to this day!!

HOW MY LIFE CHANGED AFTER BECOMING A HYPNOTHERAPIST

I hardly know where to begin with this section as so much has changed.

After completing the hypnotherapy course nearly a year ago, now my life has been enriched in many areas.

Firstly, my job as a mental health nurse continues but I now find myself in a different job. I always considered myself to be terrible at job interviews and would find the nerves kicking in several days before. But with the use of self-hypnosis and just changing the way I think about the situation I found that I was nowhere near as nervous when it came to the job interview. All skills that I picked up during my hypnotherapy training. These skills are carried forward every day in my practise as a nurse with the people that I encounter. I do not hypnotise people as such, but I have changed the language that I use, and I make positive suggestions to them and it works. Instead of focusing on negatives I try to get them to talk about positives in their lives and their strengths. We then talk about how they can use their strengths to help them with whatever their mental health difficulties may be. I am more confident in myself and this breeds confidence in them.

Secondly there is the difference in my personal life. For the first time in my life I have been able to maintain a routine of going to the gym regularly. Normally (as with most people) it is a New Year's resolution that wains by the time that I get to around March time. We are now in November and I have not missed a week yet of attendance.

Admittedly some weeks I only attend once but certainly an improvement on my usual. Regular attendance at the gym means I now feel much fitter than I did before and have lost a few lbs in weight. Not only are the physical changes but I feel better about myself and low and behold I have signed up for the Yorkshire Marathon next year. It won't be quick, and it certainly won't be pretty, but I am determined to see it through.

One area of my life that has suffered over the years is my confidence with playing music. I have had a guitar sitting gathering dust for some time and like the gym attendance I would find that I would buy the teach yourself guitar books and DVDs but would not get past the stage of building calluses on my fingers. I have now been attending classes with a guitar teacher since the middle of September and I am pleased to say that calluses are now in situ. I am loving every moment of it and have made so much more progress than ever before.

LIFE AS A HYPNOTHERAPIST

Well if you have read the above section (I take it you have or else you would probably not be reading this) you can see some of my life as a hypnotherapist. I am now a running, playing guitar, clinical hypnotherapist and I now believe that I can achieve anything that I want to achieve.

After years and years of self-doubt and lack of confidence in my own abilities and fear of taking a step outside my comfort zone this is no longer the case.

My life as a hypnotherapist is in its youth as it is less than a year since I completed the course but the immense difference in my life is immeasurable. I cannot wait to see where this path of being a clinical hypnotherapist will take me, but I tell you this I am going to enjoy every damn minute of it.

As well as enriching my own life I know that my skills are helping others from family, friends and those that come into contact with me through my work. I get the most pleasure in my life helping others and seeing the positive changes their contact with me brings. Being a hypnotherapist helps me bring about those changes and the section that follows will give you a taster of two young people that I have helped.

CLIENT SUCCESS STORY ONE

My first success story was for a young lady that was petrified of spiders. Miss B (as I shall refer to her to protect her identity) was so scared of spiders that she would find herself scanning her bedroom before retiring for the night. Miss B was living in fear that if the spiders went undiscovered she would find them dancing on her nose at some point through the night. If she saw one scurrying away in hiding she would have to sleep in another room. Miss B was worried about the effect her fear may have on her young children and decided that she needed to do something about her irrational fear.

Miss B had never had hypnotherapy before, so we talked a little about what it is and more importantly what it isn't. So, we talked about what she liked as in types of music etc. and I noted that it was clear from her appearance that she took pride in how she looked (you may feel that this is an irrelevant point, but all will be revealed further on).

So following induction and deepeners Miss B was under and I took her to a place in the country (we had talked about this in consultation) which we would further use as her place of safety. So, to cut a long story short Miss B found herself sitting in the most comfortable chair she could find listening to her favourite music when there was a knock on the door. There before Miss B was the most glamourous spider you ever did see with red lipstick and different coloured stilettos on each of her 8 feet. The spiders name was Doris (to this day I have no idea where this name come from, but it seemed to suit her image). Miss B invited Doris in who immediately began dancing to the music Miss B was playing (at this point Miss B started laughing). They then sat and had a conversation about how Miss B had nothing to fear from Doris and her kin and in fact they were much more scared of her than she was of them. Doris went on her way and I gave Miss B further time to make any changes she felt that she needed to make. We also did a usual once she wakes up she will feel much more relaxed in the company of spiders, an increase in her confidence etc.

Following a few days, I contacted Miss B for feedback and she reported that she no longer felt the need to check her room for spiders but more than this she saw a big spider the previous day and instead of feeling terrified she laughed remembering Doris and her red lippy, stilettos and dancing around the room.

CLIENT SUCCESS STORY TWO

The second success story I wish to share with you was a young man who reported always having problems with confidence and worrying what others may think of him from a young age. His confidence (or lack of it) would hold him back in life with him believing that he would not be able to go to college and complete a course in healthcare. His worrying about what others thought about him would at times get him into bother when trying to fit in with the crowd. After the initial consultation I found out that he likes running but was also into Pokémon cards. I used this knowledge during his therapy sessions.

The young man had to find his way over obstacles when on a run. With every obstacle he was able to navigate over or through his confidence would increase. He also found that his friends and family were present clapping and encouraging him along the way. I also introduced him to his own personal Pokémon card and he was able to 'power up' (I had to do my research on Pokémon's to find out information on this) on his confidence and self-esteem. I gave him time to think about changes he would like to make in his life and to think about decisions that needed to be made.

I have it on good authority that since this session with me the young man in question has now found himself at college doing an Access to Healthcare course and hopes to be going to University next year.

MY HYPNOTHERAPY PRACTICE

When setting up my practice I had real problems trying to decide upon a title to call my practice. I then came across this quote by Aristotle

'Each human being is bred with a unique set of potentials that yearn to be fulfilled as surely as the acorn yearns to become the oak within it'.

So was born 'Ancient Oak Hypnotherapy' which is based in the Cambridgeshire area.

You may be the next Jimi Hendrix waiting to be found or Mo Farah wanting to run your first marathon but not sure how to begin then please do get in touch. Seriously no matter what changes you need to make in your life or obstacles holding you back please do get in touch as hypnotherapy will help you.

If you are considering a career as a hypnotherapist then my advice is to just do it. You have absolutely nothing to lose and everything to gain.

CONTACT DETAILS:

Name:	Colleen Rea
Telephone:	(07379) 798743
Email:	colleen.hypnotherapy@outlook.com
Website:	www.colleenhypnotherapy.wixsite.com/website
Facebook:	www.facebook.com/gadgetcolleen

CARL BLACKBURN: CHESTERFIELD HYPNOTHERAPY

BEFORE BECOMING A HYPNOTHERAPIST

My name is Carl Blackburn and I am proud to be trained by Innervisions and playing my part towards Brian's Million.

Having served 24 Years in the Royal Engineers I retired from the Army with not a real thought to what I was going to do. Although I had completed certain courses to run my own instructional business delivering compliance training. This never really came to fruition. Along with the realisation that I had to now, re-adjust myself into civilian life. My personal life took a real hammering; I went through a divorce, which left me a single parent keeping my son with me. I had a lot to deal with both mentally and emotionally. I was offered a job with an educational charity working with troubled teenagers this was a tough job with some schools I worked in being very challenging. Whilst I worked for the charity this gave

me, an opportunity to complete some other training one of which stood out and helped me with the internal struggle with myself. The course was transformational coaching I was in awe of the instructor how she managed to find the underlying cause of problems and situations with the students. She had an amazing way of asking the right question allowing the student to open up and get to the route of the problem. After watching Cara the instructor, use this way of coaching that was where I thought I wanted to be. So I started on a quest to better myself.

Researching coaching questions and trying to get a better understanding of my inner self, I read self- help books and psychology books. This did help me to become a better version of me.

MY HYPNOTHERAPY TRAINING

Being an avid user of Facebook an advert kept popping up offering a taster session weekend for Hypnotherapy with a company called Innervisions. I looked at the advert a couple of times and put it to the back of my mind thinking that I don't know when I could fit that in, but something was drawing me to try it. My inner voice telling me to "give it a go". So I took the plunge and booked myself onto the next weekend that was available.

For me living in the East Midlands my training was undertaken in Sheffield in September 2016. Apprehensively I entered the room to a horseshoe arrangement of desks with several faces dotted around. Neil Woods the Innervisions Instructor and his assistant Leah (Debbie McGee) Goodall met me. I had already had a phone conversation with Neil discussing what the course entails, how it was more of seeing if the course suits you and if you are suitable for the course. There was a warm comfortable feel in the room and the group of people sat around the desks came from different backgrounds and different reasons for why they were there. At this moment in time, I did not know what to expect really. I went in with an open mind and thirst to find out what Hypnotherapy was all about. After that first day I knew that this was my calling I had to do this, the day was amazing, Neil introduced the room to Hypnosis. By the end of the session I was going to do this, "I am going to be Hypnotherapist"

This was the start of my hypnotherapy journey. That first weekend touched my inner core; it hit home, something I had been missing. All the self-help books and my past research did not fill the void that I had been missing. I have a desire to help people, a desire to better myself to become the best version of me I can be. I personally felt that Hypnosis gave me this. After the first weekend, the people that I met; my fellow Hypnotherapists became part of an extended family. Each month we would meet exchange stories of the month that had passed becoming more and more familiar with each other. I had not felt a bond like this with likeminded people since being in the armed forces.

A shared experience can bring people together in ways that cannot be found anywhere else. This was a life changing event for me, and I was sharing this with some amazing people all brought together under the Innervisions family. I also think that seeing what Neil was capable of during the sessions he seemed to have an inner sense almost like a sixth sense. His experience showed in not only his instruction but also the way he used his experience from years of practise and delivery. The demonstrations left me totally and utterly astounded at the power of the sub conscious mind.

Hypnotherapy was not something that I had considered to do, as I mentioned previously. I have always been amazed at some of the street magicians Derren Brown to me is brilliant I read his book trick of the mind and it certainly gave me food for thought. However, even that did not drive me to want to train to by a Hypnotherapist. I had been looking for something to help me develop and if so help me deal with the day-to-day stresses of life, my job and being a single parent. So when I opted to do the training weekend, the first day in the classroom we talked a lot about the how the conscious and sub conscious mind work. Sometimes against each other almost like a battle between two parts of the brain, a few demonstrations and by the first afternoon we had practised Hypnosis on fellow students and had Hypnosis done to us. Having seen this I knew straight away that this is something that I had to do. I would make the time to research everything requested of me on the course and complete all the sessions. I could sense that this was my calling. I was drawn to the advert, drawn to the company, but most of all the feeling of excitement of the journey I was about to undertake.

HOW MY LIFE CHANGED AFTER BECOMING A HYPNOTHERAPIST

So it turns out that Hypnotherapy was my calling. After the first weekend I signed up for the course, I was actually going to become a Hypnotherapist. Not once did I regret my decision from that weekend. We had different topics to try each weekend. Our challenge was to get friends and family to volunteer for the practise sessions each time I held a session something grew inside of me. The confidence and the realisation that I could actually do this. Not everyone from the first free weekend was accepted to do the course and over the following months, people would drop out for one reason or another. This was never going to happen to me. Something that I soon realised the courses I had done before I started had been to prepare me for this transition, because being a therapist is not only just about inducing Hypnosis it's so much more.

Listening to your client understanding what the subconscious is trying to tell you and how reading your client's body language can help in so many ways. Even though during my training phase, I helped quite a few of my friends and family. Self-hypnosis gave me the inner strength to accept certain changes within myself. What also soon became apparent is that its client focussed whatever worries baggage and problems you leave them at the door, active listening is so crucial to the whole session. Most of things I would do on a daily basis but with my job you never see the end result you might not even ever see the fruits of your labour come to fruition. Being a Hypnotherapist, you can see instant results and the client can leave from your session never having to worry about the issue they came to you with. Almost like a miracle happening before your eyes. Helping the client achieve what they want, and that's why I became a Hypnotherapist.

CLIENT SUCCESS STORY ONE

A memorable success for me was the, first person I ever hypnotised; this was another student on the course. He was quiet and unassuming he had not been relaxed the whole day and seemed tense and uptight. I gave him a confidence boost and suggested that he could do anything he put his mind too. Each month after that session, the student and I talked and got to know each other really well. His transformation through the course was astounding.

He lost weight, he gained confidence and each month he would come into the room more and more confident this was noticed by the rest of the group how much he had grown in confidence. I would complement him on his achievements and each time we talked, he would tell me that his achievements were down to our session from that first weekend. He would tell me "it's down to you this". I cannot take credit for your awesome transformation I just helped you to see what was already inside of you. We are still in touch and I am proud to call him my friend.

CLIENT SUCCESS STORY TWO

Another success that stands out is a friend of mine he had been suffering from chest pains and been to the doctors. He had gone through several tests an ECG, a scan and blood test. All the results had come back as normal with nothing unusual recorded. Nevertheless, he was still suffering with the chest pains he would get these quite often throughout the week. Other than this he was quite fit and healthy a non-smoker and around 47 years old. I said to him come, see me, and see what we can do. Quite sceptical he said I doubt you can hypnotise me but I will try it. He was actually quite easy and followed my suggestions quite well. He has been pain free ever since. He is, a now convert and a great advocate for my business.

MY HYPNOTHERAPY PRACTICE

After my graduation, I had looked into many ways of how I could integrate hypnotherapy into my life. Not an easy thing to do as I have a full time job and a young son to support. In an ideal world, I would have quit my job and gone full time but I have to live with reality and this was never going to be a workable solution. Having no financial backer I had done all this so far with my monthly wage. I was not in any financial situation to take that plunge. My life as a Hypnotherapist is part time. I have converted my garage into a therapy suit. I see clients on a basis that can fit into my work/parent life. I take each client on what their needs are and adjust my diary to make sure I can see them a soon as possible. This is restricted sometimes to the weekend but for me to ensure that the practise grows I need to build a database and word of mouth referrals. Whenever there is a lull in the practise, I research my client's situations and try out different techniques. I also look into how to develop my practise further. However, the thing that still drives me the most is the want to help people Hypnotherapy is part of my life now and I do not ever see it not being there. My vision for the future is not having my practise in my converted garage but to have it running out of a centre alongside other therapists all working under the same roof. Almost like a centre of excellence. Chesterfield Hypnotherapy is a small client focussed Hypnotherapy practise based in the town of Chesterfield on the edge of the Peak District. I am a registered Hypnoslimmer consultant, I offer smoking cessation, help with fears, phobias, anxiety and stress. What I strive to give my clients is the tools and confidence to unlock their true potential, bettering themselves in every way possible.

CONTACT

Name: Carl Blackburn
Telephone: (07901) 003966
Email: carlblackburn@chesterfield-hypnotherapy.com
Website: chesterfield-hypnotherapy.com
Facebook: www.facebook.com/carl.blackburn.9847

CHARLOTTE GILL: HALCYON HYPNOTHERAPY

BEFORE BECOMING A HYPNOTHERAPIST

I had never had a clue what I wanted to do as a "grown up". My career preferences changed with the wind. I do remember toying with the ideas of being a forensic criminologist or whatever it was Robbie Coltrane portrayed in the TV series "Cracker" A journalist, an MP, and doctor and so on. When it came to actually committing to a life path, that was easier said than done. I breezed through my GCSE's and was doing fine with my A-levels at 17yrs old before quitting halfway through to study travel and tourism instead. I ditched English (boring), German (too laborious) and Psychology (I couldn't get my head around the fact that Freud was liked and respected despite his bizarre theories) and I opted for adventure instead.

I did really well in the tourism industry, naturally extroverted and great with people, I travelled, I worked as a rep in the Algarve and loved the adventure, until I realised how little money was to be earned that way and I hot-footed it back to blighty and went to university. I undertook a health science access course to get my foot in the door and was set on becoming a nurse until I realised there was a long wait to get onto the course I needed so I emailed the clearing officials and was offered a Science Teaching Degree with immediate start. That was good enough for me and I was in. I guess I've always believed in 'fate' and I never really worried about where I would end up however. I did feel the weight of time upon my shoulders and a need to kind of 'catch up' or 'be where I should be' within a certain time at that point.

Not one to make things easy for myself I became pregnant and bought a house with my partner within the first academic year. I was 24. My gorgeous son was born very conveniently in the summer holidays and I continued straight into my second year. Little did I know what I was dealing with in my personal life at that time I juggled working full time for my friend as a Personal Assistant, a very toxic relationship with a sociopath, and my studies alongside being a first time mum. Looking back I don't know how I did it. I just did. Failure wasn't ever an option for me and I think it was almost a manic phase, fuelled by adrenaline and stress that got me through it. I was pregnant again within 5 months of having my son and this time I did take a year out, moved away from the unhappy family home, set up a new life on my own with the addition of a beautiful new baby daughter and carried on at 100 miles per hour. I regularly fell asleep on the bedroom floor, singing the little ones to sleep at 7pm and woke up later to work through the night planning lessons. I feel I missed out a lot on the children's little milestones, walking, first words etc. However no one could have loved them as much as my Nanan Pat without whom none of it would have been possible and we shared the responsibility of their upbringing. It was actually a very happy time. I adjusted to the speed and intensity with which my life was flowing and spent every free moment with the little ones. I swear they have forgotten more days out than most children have even had, they were spoiled to death and if I am honest "over compensated" for my guilt at leaving them with Nanan so much to study.

I loved teaching I was good at it and I loved the challenges that working with teenagers brought. What I didn't like however, was the fact that during my placement year. I had hardly blinked and the year was over. My life sped by so quickly and I suddenly realised that the next 40 or so years of my life might do the same if I were to continue working in formal education. I really could not do that to my children. I could sacrifice a couple of years as a means to an end but I wanted to be the one who took them to school and picked them up afterwards. I wanted to attend school days out and watch every performance they appeared in so I made the decision to private tutor instead. Best thing I'd ever done up until that point.

I got married at 29yrs of age and had a third cheeky little monkey my second daughter and plodded along for a while however it wasn't enough for me. I loved tutoring. However I needed more mental stimulation for myself. I booked on to the Innervisions School of Clinical Hypnosis FREE Foundation weekend course.

MY HYPNOTHERAPY TRAINING

From the very first weekend with Neil Woods, the tutor responsible for the Sheffield area, I knew that I wanted to become a Hypnotherapist and that nothing was going to stop me. I originally attended the free part of the course with my best friend and we both decided to continue, quickly setting up our clinic together from about halfway through the course and learning by experience as we went along.

We had been having the odd difference in opinion as to how we ran the business and I was a little dubious of her motivations for choosing Hypnotherapy as her career. I wanted to help people and to discover more and more about the human mind and her sights appeared to be more fixed on the financial outcome. Then the strangest thing happened. I had a tarot card reading in which it was predicted that this business relationship would end. The reader foretold that I would be wanted on the course and that my friend would not. Part of me believed that it was a possibility but I wasn't fully convinced until it happened exactly as predicted. During a conversation with Brian Glenn, who is principal of Innervisions, my best friend of 10 years made a completely unacceptable judgemental and prejudiced comment about the other students in her class which saw her swiftly asked to leave the course as she was not considered to be the type of person fit to be an Innervisions graduate. I was gobsmacked as I stood there realising what was unfolding and of course I then had to choose to continue on the course or to defend her and leave. I was never in doubt. There was no way I was going to quit and the fact that it had been predicted six months before just strengthened my resolve. She left and I never saw her again. We spoke maybe three times on the phone to arrange practicalities of dissolving the business partnership; however she decided we could no longer be friends. I put my absolute all into my training despite my relationship crumbling at home as my new found positivity and zest for life seemed to take us in different directions. I ultimately "lost" my best friend and my Husband in the process of becoming a Hypnotherapist. However looking back I believe that my new perspective simply allowed me to see these people for what they really were and in reality I "lost" nothing at all. In fact I actually found myself and realised my true worth aged 32.

HOW MY LIFE CHANGED AFTER BECOMING A HYPNOTHERAPIST

Prior to beginning my training I had been diagnosed with PTSD from my previous abusive relationship and ultimately depression. I was prescribed anti-depressants which made me gain weight and stop caring about anything. From the first weekend I attended the hypnotherapy training course I knew I was on the right path and I binned the pills. I was high on the mental stimulation, learning about the law of attraction and the positivity which being around other open-minded people was bringing. I rejected negativity completely, I stopped listening to sad songs, I cut negative people from my life and grew so much as a person. I stopped worrying about what I was 'supposed' to be doing or what others thought of me and I began to completely trust in the universe and what my true purpose should be. I felt like I was doing the right thing and that was enough. Sadly my husband (who was previously the positive one between us by a mile) just didn't support me emotionally at all. I had supported him through many challenges I tutored him through re-taking his GCSE Math, I supported him through redundancy and re -training for a new career, I did the admin for him in self-employment ventures and he was not interested in the slightest about my new career direction. He didn't want to listen to what I'd been learning or finding out or even to try it for himself or anything. I thought a lot about my decision to leave him. To the outside world we were the "golden couple". Everything appeared to be perfect we had beautiful children good careers and all that jazz. Ultimately it was the promise that I had made to myself to no longer tolerate negativity in my life that I had to remain true to. And I left.

MY HYPNOTHERAPY TRAINING

My inspiration and motivation to train stems from my own experiences of Hypnotherapy in the past. Prior to my marriage I had put on weight and I had hypnotherapy for weight-loss and it really worked I was soon running 10k at the weekends for fun and was at the peak of my physical fitness. The biggest change however was the uplift in mood that I felt. My Hypnotherapist gave me some really confidence boosting suggestions and I lapped them up. I left the room bouncing and for the first time in my life saw the world through the eyes of an optimist. She gave me her copy of 'The secret' by Rhonda Byrne and opened my eyes to the Law of attraction, something I absolutely live my life by now. I returned for a further session regarding letting go of my emotional ties to my ex - I just couldn't shake a sense of responsibility that I felt for him no matter how despicable he treated me and I was essentially still a puppet in his show. I engaged in the incessant arguing I believed his insults and put downs and I could not cut him off, until I had hypnotherapy. After just one session I felt absolutely nothing! I felt absolutely nothing towards him, I found a peaceful ambivalence and I was fascinated I needed to understand how Hypnotherapy can be so powerful. I actually left my last session owing £5 (due to her not having the correct change) and due to how quickly things went from there I never returned as a client so I still owed the money about 3 years later. As soon as I qualified I sent a bouquet of flowers and a note explaining my gratitude to her for the inspiration along with the fiver, I probably owed some interest by then however I think were square enough now.

CLIENT SUCCESS STORY ONE

Over the past three years I have worked with hundreds of clients. I am gradually narrowing my areas of focus as I go however I began so enthusiastically that I just wanted to use hypnotherapy for EVERYTHING. As a result I have worked with such an interesting range of conditions and issues that it is difficult to choose a favourite. I guess my heart lies with anxiety clients as my high energy and unshakable positivity always seems to have a great effect and to see a sad troubled face turn into a smiley bright one over just a couple of sessions make it magical to me. My most extreme example is a lady who was suffering really badly from anxiety to the point that she could hardly speak to me through her tears and confessed that she had on occasion felt suicidal despite having an apparently "nice" life, loving husband and children etc. on the outside. A good clear-out of the subconscious cobwebs and mega confidence boosting later she called to cancel her third session as she was completely happy with her outlook on life. She even remained calm and unbothered when her son dropped his iPhone into a lake (something which would previously send her spiralling into despair) she didn't give a stuff! I see her posts on Facebook from time to time and I know that she is living a full and adventurous life. This is one client I am so proud of.

CLIENT SUCCESS STORY TWO

Another client that particularly warms my heart is one of my little hypo-tuition girls. I say girl, she is 16 and this is a recent one. The whole family mum dad and daughter came to see me and explained that this usually bright confident intelligent school girl had over the past year or so become less and less enthused about learning. So much so that she was spending hours staring at her revision books and taking nothing in. Naturally she was freaking out about the fast upcoming exams. I tutored her through her GCSE math and she passed with flying colours in the end. However the really interesting part was in the beginning. I used hypnotherapy to discover where the "symptoms" stemmed from. We switched up the confidence and focus as well as doing some gentle digging to discover the source. On the second session we had a breakthrough. It was such a beautiful moment when it was discovered that the younger girl had thoroughly enjoyed her dad's level of involvement in her learning. Dad was clearly a very concerned and loving parent the great relationship between them was apparent from the moment I met them. Mum worked tirelessly to support her in her dreams of becoming a star one day and the family as a unit were just great. The problem (which none of them had even realised was the problem) lay in the fact that as an older child a teenager no less, the daughter had been given more space and the assumption was that she no longer needed her parental input academically. And part of her really missed that. So I, grinning like a Cheshire cat, relayed this information to dad who was more than happy to feature more prominently in his daughter's revision. It was agreed that he would help out by testing her knowledge etc. and she would receive the positive feedback of impressing her father by really knowing her stuff. This child went from borderline despair to being my most avid student. From shying away from exam questions to actively seeking out more and more difficult questions to challenge her. We were working on questions that were over and above the level necessary for her GCSE grade needed and she begged her parents for more and more tuition as she enjoyed learning once again. She has now secured a place in a prestigious performing arts college and is well on her way to becoming famous, of that I have no doubt.

LIFE AS A HYPNOTHERAPIST

I won't lie the first year and a half setting up my business was very tough going. I had to somehow make it work and around the school run which gave me a mere 4.5 hours a day. I began by using my working tax credits from tutoring to pay rent on my first clinic and I then had to earn the rent back before I even begun to make profit. My private tutoring kept me afloat and I could always see the bigger picture. Factoring in additional costs such as my subscriptions and advertising, leaflets, bills, signage on the clinic, website costs I basically worked for nothing for about the first year. As a single mother of three, I set up on a shoestring with no capital to outlay and I've had to take my time and do as much for myself as possible. Outsourcing the work was not a financially viable option. I swapped skills with a local man who in return for hypnotherapy, taught me and helped me to create, build and SEO my website. I learned how to do all of that myself and spent night after night working on the behind the scenes stuff and building the foundations of my business. When my children were poorly I had no sick pay, and I was basically earning less than being on the dole. All of this as well as actually still learning the ropes as I was by no means as experienced as I wanted to be yet. It got to around November, I had literally gotten down to my last pair of jeans and they were faded with a hole in them before everything turned around. I had a great Christmas and business took off so much I decided to open a second clinic in the City Centre. Obviously this ate into my newly acquired profits but as I saw it I was moving forwards.

A period of sickness made me realise how difficult working alone was and there was an element of loneliness that I just couldn't shake. I got the idea of a collaborative effort and sought out other Innervisions trained hypnotherapists to work alongside me. One of my clients was so inspired by her therapy that she too decided to train as a hypnotherapist. And now I am part of something really special. Myself and three other Hypnotherapists, as well as a holistic therapist work together to offer a wide variety of services from hypnotherapy to massage, reiki, EFT, past life regression, law of attraction and much more. I still privately tutor however with a twist. I market myself towards clients who do not want a basic education for their child, or children with barriers to learning. I use my hypnotherapist skill set to work with each learner to develop confidence, improve focus, combat exam stress and deepen understanding of the subject. This is my main specialist area and I am grateful that I can use my degree in teaching to do real good. I feel that I offer learners a second chance to realise their potential and their worth it, is truly magical. When I am ill my work partners cover me and vice versa, we support each other and chat daily, meeting up at least weekly and working on larger scale projects as a team. I really could not envision myself doing anything other than this. I work the hours I choose to and have an amazing work / life balance.

MY HYPNOTHERAPY PRACTICE

Currently, I am the owner of Halcyon Hypnotherapy and Advanced Learning in Sheffield. I have a large gorgeous clinic in Stockbridge and a smaller clinic in an ultramodern business centre in Sheffield City centre. My work partners are like family and we refer clients between ourselves according to our strengths so that each client receives the best possible therapy or combination of therapies for them. We support each other and motivate each other in every way. My former client has recently qualified and the family continues to grow. We work together on joint projects and keep each other sane. I feel we offer an unmatched level of variety and choice for Sheffield clients which is a strength as no one size fits all. There are many plans for events and soon we will begin to offer training to others in our specialist areas, this will be a natural extension of our growing success. This is very much only the beginning.

General Hypnotherapy Register
Acknowledged Supervisor

I have recently been given the honour of becoming Innervisions official General Hypnotherapy Register acknowledged supervision officer which means that I can now play a bigger part in helping, guiding and hopefully inspiring other new hypnotherapists to fulfil their potential. I have every aspiration to teach Hypnotherapy one day too, however even though my average pace is 100mph it's got to be one step at a time for me and I feel I will be ready for that next step when I have around 5 years of experience behind me. I want to write books too after about ten years or so. That is one of the most delightful realisations that I have had. The fact that this is a career I won't become too old and infirm to continue. In actual fact, age and experience will make me a BETTER hypnotherapist with more authority to actually have an opinion and hopefully one day people will want to read what I have to write and listen to what I have to say. So I can advance towards old age in the assurance that my beloved career will grow and mature with me.

Thank you for taking the time to read my story.

CONTACT DETAILS:

Name: Charlotte Gill
Telephone: (07788) 230304
Email: halcyonhypno1@gmail.com
Website: www.halcyonhypnotherapysheffield.com
Facebook: www.facebook.com/halcyonhypnotherapysheffield

THE DARKER SIDE

I (Brian) would like to introduce you to Donna Jenkinson, one of our senior tutors with a role here in Spain. Donna and I recently experienced vicious and unjustified character attacks from a group of people living here in Spain. I asked Donna to write about her experience by way of balancing the positive and negative aspects of being a hypnotherapist. May I add that as a result of this, we are as a company much stronger due to this negative experience and we are proud to continue to be the top training provider in UK and Spain.

DONNA JENKINSON: INNERVISIONS TUTOR – SPAIN

I personally never set out to become a hypnotherapist. Growing up working in a typical 'nine to five' accounts environment I was on many occasions told that I am a natural healer, followed by "you will be a great philosopher" somehow stunned and confused me. Yet I followed the signs that drew me into this world and walked through the doors that opened, and found myself in this most gratifying, enriching and rewarding life-changing career!

Just a few years ago I was in that typical work environment and thought I had acquired everything that I was told was required to create my dream life. A nice home, nice car, loving husband and family. Yet still I felt unhappy, I felt disconnected, and had no idea about my 'real' purpose.

I had always had an interest and fascination towards psychology and the mind to some degree, and people always warmed to me with their concerns and problems and I knew instinctively what to say! Without realising it I was putting a smile on their faces. This gave me such a warm wonderful feeling. I did consider on a number of occasions to apply for a counselling course but something stopped and held me back and I couldn't understand what. Now I realise that counselling was not meant to be as it would have obviously conflicted with the path that was mapped out for me.

Since high school, I regularly suffered from IBS. I took just about every medication known and suffered from this very debilitating illness. This continued and in later life eventually led me to regular colonic irrigations to ease the discomfort and clear out the backed up waste, fluid and toxins that were stored and continued to poison my body.

This is I then where I discovered hypnotherapy. The complimentary health centre I was attending to deal with my IBS was advertising a free hypnotherapy training weekend. Without question, I signed up to attend the course, did the free weekend and had no doubt whatsoever that I had to continue the training to practitioner level!

I am thrilled to say that just one of the many side effects of completing the hypnotherapy course (coupled with a couple of sessions), helped me completely rid this horrible illness, which I was told by the doctor to put up with and have to live with for the rest of my life and when we are given a 'label' from a doctor this sticks and I readily accepted ownership of this!

Seeing so many changes quickly within myself, ridding this terrible illness once and for all as well as saving the regular fees on the colonic treatments and medication, my eagerness and fascination grew and I quickly became very immersed in this field. My passion was recognised and I was very soon asked to shadow one of our leading tutors to train and eventually become a tutor myself. A proposition coming from our tutor, Brian Glenn who is principal of Innervisions School of Clinical Hypnosis made me immensely proud. And so now as a practicing hypnotherapist as well as a tutor for one of the UK's leading training providers, I can provide that same enriching experience for my clients as well as share the skills with our students, who in turn open my mind to vast wisdom and rich experiences.

And so my own experiences with hypnosis took me deep into my higher consciousness where I could discover who I was and what I was meant to do with my life as well as learn an independent career and create a lifestyle that gave me flexibility. I soon realised this is the career choice where I could leave MY positive mark on the world!

NOW I am excited to get up and go to work, I am thrilled to see clients come to my office concerned about their continual health issues and leave with peace and purpose in their hearts. When I realised I could gain a deeper understanding of humanity, transform lives, and create permanent positive results for people I was hooked and finally realised this is how I would make a difference in the world. I just wasn't sure how this would have come about, but once I stepped into the world of hypnotherapy, the possibilities were wide open to me!

In the beginning, it did seem like a daunting task to be the one to make such needed changes. But soon I realised that with the techniques I taught my clients, would show the way to their own healing and would be delighted with their rapid transformation. So for me, it is a deep honour to play a part in the lives of so many people and to fulfil my destiny in making such a valuable difference in the world.

Every single day I feel blessed and privileged to have this role in life. I live and breathe this stuff, continuing to study, research and learn as much as I possibly can. Then gratitude finally turned in my favour when I was promoted and given the opportunity to move to Spain and continue my work as Innervisions tutor!

Not only was I blessed with such wonderful work and wonderful people in the UK, (some of whom who will remain lifelong and very dear friends) but now to work with and teach people from all parts of the world in Spain!

At the same time, life took a sad turn for me when my marriage ended and I chose to leave the marital home. Knowing what I know in the field of hypnosis, I understood that the problems I had with my husband were mine and not his. I cannot change him, it is not my right to do so, and so I had to make the decision to change something for me. I packed up my little mini and began my adventure with a five-hour drive to Portsmouth to board the overnight ferry to Spain. It was the early afternoon when I arrived in Spain and still, I had a further nine-hour hour drive to what was to become my new home and life!

Driving away from my home in the UK was one of the scariest and of course saddest moments of my life. Yet gradually an overwhelming feeling of freedom and excitement took over! I had done something I never believed I could ever have the confidence to do. All these changes evolved as part of my own experiences due to my own emotional intelligence being strengthened and nurtured, all thanks to hypnosis.

All of a sudden my wings spread and I was free. Butterflies are hugely significant to me and play a very important part in my life; as those who know me know only too well. I am now that butterfly!

Life here in Spain was wonderful, I quickly adapted to life here and began to find my way to be a part of an ever-growing, thriving network of other hypnotherapists. This also should have been an exciting time for me; as we all have our own qualities, strengths and different skill sets that we can contribute in our own ways.

Whilst this book is all about positive and inspiring experiences, I was given the opportunity to share my recent experience of the downside to this profession.

Innervisions and I became victims of bullies, to the point of almost being driven out of Spain. We were continually bullied and intimidated by a handful of people, some with big egos, who clearly were not coming from a good place. These people are supposed to be ethical and moral hypnotherapists!

This went on for almost a year. Throughout that time I remained quiet, sat back and took all the insults and accusations thrown at us. I got up every morning, held my head high, knowing that everything I do continues to come from my heart. With the support of dear friends and family, I got through a terrible situation that almost finished and destroyed me, my dream and Innervisions.

It saddens me deeply to know that there are people out here in Spain whom I classed as wonderful and supportive friends, colleagues and associates, that I shared particularly sensitive, personal moments with, and I will ALWAYS be grateful for their support and kind words of encouragement that would often overwhelm me. Yet these people, when things did not go their way, turned completely against me with such nasty and vicious attacks both personally and professionally. This affected the courses I was running, as our students were poisoned and enticed away right from us at any and all opportunity. Countless lies and slanderous comments were spread. At one point we took legal advice, but we decided not to pursue that route as this was not what I came to Spain for nor expected, so we decided to take a more loving option to getting ourselves back on track!

It was a very devastating time and words failed me, and I cannot describe how it felt to all of a sudden, almost overnight, have an army of enemies! Something I have never encountered ever before in my life and didn't know how to deal with it.

The obvious and instinctive thing to do would have been to retaliate and fight back. But we all remained calm put on a very brave face and continued each day knowing as long as we were genuine, spoke only the truth then the universe will look after us and the outcome would speak for itself.

By this time my confidence was destroyed, I went from getting up every morning feeling blessed and looking forward to what new opportunities the day brought, to dreading getting out of bed and waiting to find what was going to hit us next.

I thought I was coping well, putting on a brave face for my family and ongoing students. But this negative stuff affected me emotionally and physically even with my barriers up my sub conscious tore them down, I was mortified... Hair Loss! My hair had started falling out in small clumps.

Adding to the emotional and physical blow there was also added stress that my income had dropped drastically, at the time when I was helping financially support my daughter and new-born grandson living with me. This should have been a time where I was able to enjoy those precious first months being a grandma. It has taken a very long time for me to come to terms with and forgive myself for not being able to enjoy and focus on them while they were staying here with me. A time that should have been so precious, but was stolen from me due to all the stress and battling events that occurred. A time that I can never get back and have again. But hey, the best is yet to come!

The stress eventually took its toll, so my daughter and grandson flew back to the UK to relieve the financial burden from me. For me it was a very sad and devastating time to watch them go, leaving me feeling helpless and useless.

Fortunately, I am blessed with two very understanding and amazing daughters who have continued to support me whilst at the same time learn to grow up very quickly and become independent. They make me so proud! They encouraged me to stay here in Spain as they believe I was drawn here for a reason. They are happy to remain in the UK for now until such a time that they can return.

Fortunately, things have now quietened down here in Spain, but not completely. (still the odd rattle now and again). Despite all of the challenges we faced we are still here and now getting stronger and stronger by the moment. For me, I accept this was a lesson and all part of a bigger journey. The overwhelming support from friends, colleagues and students have brought me to tears many times, and they have reminded me just how genuine and sincere I am. I know as long as I continue to come from a genuine place of love I will go far!

I will always be grateful to each and every one who has stood by us and believed in us. As I continue to read my ever-growing compilation of testimonies and feedback, the poems written and dedicated to me and also books dedicated to us for assisting in the changes in these peoples lives.

Finally, as we all know, forgiveness is a very powerful tool and one that I have applied to each and every one who has affected me. This has taught me that forgiveness works and now I do feel good about myself again. To learn how to self-heal has given me my self-empowerment and my self-control back and that's a wonderful feeling.

As well as continuing my role as Spain's Ambassador for Innervisions School of Clinical Hypnosis, and senior tutor, I am now also part of a wonderful clinic I share with another hypnotherapist, Peter Warke and we are building up business together and seeing clients. I am also keeping myself busy writing presentations, doing workshops and just really looking forward to raising the awareness and spreading the word of hypnotherapy; how it transforms lives, to help reach that all-important million that is Brian Glenn's dream.

As I do live and breathe this and don't think I ever really switch off. One of the things that makes me smile inside, and what I love about Peter, is that I see so many traits in him that remind me of myself having the passion and drive with this profession. So I know he will go far and be very successful and so look forward to a very exciting and successful working relationship with him, and work with and involve the local Spanish community.

I am also now part of a wonderful charity who support single and lone women here in Spain struggling with the challenges due to financial hardship or relationship break ups/issues and I feel so grateful to be able to contribute and give back.

So to sum up, life is now back on track and more positive and optimistic than ever before, I always encourage our students to go out there and not necessarily expect to see a miracle but to be somebodies miracle. And when I think back to my own experiences I can recall some wonderful people of whom I have had the privilege of working with.

I will always remember a special lady who one evening I was treating for confidence and OCD issues. On finishing the session, she reached the door to leave and broke down in floods of tears. Well, clients are meant to leave feeling somewhat more positive not sad. So I called her back, sat her down and comfort her!

She proceeded to tell me she was scared. Scared that the cancer was going to come back! She went on to explain that she had cancer at a very young age as a child she had spent a lot of time in hospital having her treatment. Despite being in remission for 10 years she had this fear it was now going to come back.

What was interesting is that she had this journal that she kept. She had written about her experiences and events. Knowing what we know, if you continue to keep such information and re-read you are keeping the issue very much alive and strengthening/reinforcing those negative neuro pathways.

I proceeded with a technique to quickly extinguish and neutralise those feelings which she could only describe as a roller coaster and she left my office immediately feeling more calm and relaxed smiling.
I then got a message later that week from her mother, thanking me. She said that she didn't know what I had done, but that evening her daughter had turned up at her house, lit the barbecue in the back garden and threw the journal on and burned it! I felt elated this girl finally let this fear go and she went on to find the strength to work in supporting and helping others who have similar experiences.

Another wonderful person who comes to mind that will stay with me I can recall is a lady who came along for weight control. She was also stuck and discontented with her work and needed help in career decisions to help her move forward. We commenced with the regular hypnoslimmer sessions in which time she reduced her weight and shape nicely and not exercising before indirectly started to actively walk, run, dance and do Zumba and become much physically more active than she ever recalls!

Out of the blue this lady was then struck down with cancer which was just absolutely shocking and devastating. Privately and very bravely she worked her way through this time in which she believes her very positive mindset coupled with her better physical health helped her through this situation in which she made a full and surprisingly quick recovery.

This lady was an inspiration, so brave and strong but undoubtedly knew her way through it, was this new and positive outlook on life, she was just this bundle of joy and positivity! Eventually, she did go onto a new career and the last time I caught up with her, she was at her fittest and this vibrant positive 'self' shined through and that was just so wonderful to see, as maybe I played a little part in those changes...

So it is a huge honour me to contribute towards this book and could simply not miss this opportunity. Thank you for reading.

CONTACT

Name: Donna Jenkinson
Telephone: (+34) 603283999
Email: donnawood1711@yahoo.co.uk
Website: www.donnajenkinson.es
Facebook: www.facebook.com/donna.zekavica

ADDENDUM

I would like to thank all our contributors to this book and also thank each and every person who has contributed to making the world a better place via our unique teachings.

I have absolutely no idea how close I am to achieving my million right now. Obviously it's something that is impossible to count! But I strive daily for that million. What I can tell you though is that my Karma is now good and fantastic things are happening to me. From living in Woolworths shop doorways a few years ago to living the dream in sunny Spain I feel I must now be doing something right!

Harnessing the potential of the laws of attraction help too!

Special thanks to one of my besties, Kathryn Laing for her kind words in the acknowledgement section of this book.

I urge you to enjoy being who and what you have become. And if you want to make a significant difference to this world, then be that difference!

Being **YOU** is the only way to truly live.

You must be what it is that you're seeking. In this universe of attraction and energy, you can't have a desire to attract a mate who's confident, generous, non-judgmental, and gentle, and expect that desire to be manifested if you're thinking and acting in non-confident, selfish, judgmental, or arrogant ways.

Spend time with nice people who are smart, driven, kind, caring, considerate, compassionate and likeminded. Choose friends who you are proud to know, people you admire, who love and respect you, people who make your day a little brighter simply by being in it.

Relationships should help you, not hurt you.

Surround yourself with people who reflect the person you want to be.

Life is too short to spend time with people who suck the happiness out of you. When you free yourself from negative people, you free yourself to be YOU – and being YOU is the only way to truly live.

Don't live your life with hate in your heart. You will end up hurting yourself more than the people you hate.

Forgiveness is not saying, "What you did to me is okay." It is saying, "I'm not going to let what you did to me ruin my happiness anymore."

Forgiveness is the remedy. It doesn't mean you're erasing the past, or forgetting what happened. It means you're letting go of the resentment and pain, and choosing to learn from the incident and move on with your life.

Remember, the less time you spend hating the people who hurt you, the more time you'll have to love the people who love you.

Wishing you love, peace and continued happiness.

Keep on keeping on!

Brian Glenn
PRINCIPAL
INNERVISIONS SCHOOL OF CLINICAL HYPNOSIS
www.innervisionsuk.com

INNERVISIONS SCHOOL OF CLINICAL HYPNOSIS

Established in 1996, Innervisions School of Clinical Hypnosis is the training provider of choice providing specialised training in modern clinical hypnosis. And with 21 years of training experience behind us, we are now one of the UK's leading training providers.

We aim to be the best in our particular field and to surpass our student's expectations; our teaching methods are unique, supportive, warm and friendly. We are dedicated to this profession and we intend to assist and train each and every student to become a competent practitioner in modern clinical hypnosis and hypnotherapy.

The course is designed to be of particular relevance to those in the caring profession as well as anyone who has an interest in the field of human potential and personal development. Whilst academic qualifications may be an advantage, we regard it as only being a small part of the learning curve to becoming a competent clinical hypnotherapist. This hypnotherapy training course is therefore open to those with a genuine interest in hypnotherapy irrespective of race, religion, and environmental classification, even though they may not have any relevant prior learning or training.

A UNIQUE OPPORTUNITY TO TRAIN FOR A REWARDING NEW CAREER

For two exciting days, Discover Hypnotherapy with our world class tutors and find out if hypnotherapy is the right career for you. You are invited to apply for a FREE place on our foundation weekend. Absolutely 100% free and unconditional.

www.innervisionsuk.com

ACCREDITATION

Our hypnotherapy training courses are fully supported and accredited by the General Hypnotherapy Standards Council.

Our practitioner level training course has been assessed and validated at practitioner level by The General Hypnotherapy Standards Council (UK). Graduates are eligible for professional registration with The General Hypnotherapy Register at full practitioner status.

The GHSC was a key participant within the Working Group for Hypnotherapy Regulation whose primary purpose was to facilitate agreed standards within the profession and to subsequently bring about Voluntary Self-regulation (VSR), an officially recognised status, for the entire industry. To facilitate this, the Group actively co-operated with other industry representatives within the Hypnotherapy Regulatory Forum (a body established by the now defunct Prince's Foundation for Integrated Health) and as a consequence VSR was finally established via the Natural Healthcare Council (CNHC) set up in 2008 with Department of Health funding - when it admitted Hypnotherapy into its regulatory system on 1st December 2010.

DIPLOMA

Our Diploma in Hypnotherapy and Psychotherapy has been validated by the General Hypnotherapy Standards Council (GHSC) and Graduates from this course are eligible for professional registration with the General Hypnotherapy Register (the GHSC's registering agency) at full Practitioner status, together with the acquisition of the industry based award - the General Qualification in Hypnotherapy Practice (GQHP).

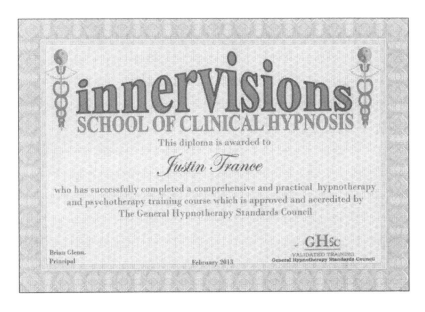

Graduates of this course will also be eligible to register with the Complementary and Natural Healthcare Council (CNHC). For more information visit **www.cnhc.org.uk**

For two exciting days, Discover Hypnotherapy with our world class tutors and find out if hypnotherapy is the right career for you. You are invited to apply for a FREE place on our foundation weekend. Absolutely 100% free and unconditional.

www.**innervisionsuk**.com

CONTRIBUTORS

Name: Gaynor Marie Duffy
Telephone: (07443) 424293
Email: gaynor@betransformation.com
Website: www.betransformation.com

Name: Peter Wall
Telephone: (07973) 736511
Email: peter.wall@live.co.uk
Website: www.innerlight-hypnosis.com

Name: Steven Smith
Telephone: (07432) 464960
Email: info@scshypnosis.com
Website: www.scshypnosis.com

Name: Les Roberts
Telephone: (07464) 099447
Email: lesrobertshypno@sky.com

Name: Amanda Hopper
Telephone: (07729) 195559
Email: info@amandahopperhypnotherapy.co.uk
Website: www.amandahopperhypnotherapy.co.uk

Name: Peter Warke
Telephone: (+34) 602 21 55 18
Email: peterwarke@hotmail.com

Name: Colleen Rea
Telephone: (07379) 798743
Email: colleen.hypnotherapy@outlook.com
Website: www.colleenhypnotherapy.wixsite.com/website

Name: Charlotte Gill
Telephone: (07788) 230304
Email: halcyonhypno1@gmail.com
Website: www.halcyonhypnotherapysheffield.com

Name: Hilary Moulds
Telephone: (07721) 652440
Email: enquiries@hilarymoulds.com
Website: www.hilarymoulds.com

Name: Laura Shewfelt
Telephone: (07931) 799025
Email: hello@yourweightlossfairy.com
Website: www.yourweightlossfairy.com

Name: Tee Liburd
Telephone: (07828) 231129
Email: hello@togethernesstherapy.co.uk
Website: www.togethernesstherapy.co.uk

Name: Donna Jenkinson
Telephone: (+34) 603283999
Email: donnawood1711@yahoo.co.uk
Website: www.donnajenkinson.es

Name: Carl Blackburn
Telephone: (07901) 003966
Email: carlblackburn@chesterfield-hypnotherapy.com
Website: chesterfield-hypnotherapy.com

I surrender my fear and replace it with love,

I surrender my doubt and replace it with confidence,

I see myself moving out into the world with ease and I give thanks for all I learn and experience

Each new day is full of infinite possibilities!

Printed in Great Britain
by Amazon